Preface

Life can be tedious, exacting and overwhelming. At these times I fantasized boarding an airplane, traveling from city to city that I fancied, staying until I had seen all the sights, and then continuing around the world. My fantasy was not far-fetched because I was authorized to fly, space available, on US Airways by my son Greg, a pilot instructor in Charlotte, North Carolina.

I was ecstatic when I retired. My career had been fulfilling as a guidance counselor, but now I could set my own agenda. True, I would have to modify my vision. Wild thoughts suddenly entered my mind, such as, "I do not have to listen to everything that others say. I can daydream or frown or doze off. I don't have to smile at bothersome people or agree more than I would like. I can go back to bed without calling in sick if I am tired. I can go out for breakfast and lunch and dinner. I don't have to sit through boring meetings or listen to abusive parents or administrators. I don't have to worry if Johnny can't read. I can chew gum all day and talk on the phone as often as I like. I can put my feet up, watch my favorite TV program, and eat chocolates. With this in mind, I decided that the best was yet to come.

Then reality set in. What would I do with my time when I retired? The answer was simple when I considered my values. First, I would complete the Bible Study Fellowship Program. Second, I would spend more time with family. Third, I would travel the world and see all that I could. Fourth, I would take oil and watercolor lessons and "paint myself silly". Fifth, I would join a tennis group.

My second concern was who would accompany me on my travels, since my husband was not retired. A bridge player friend said, “That’s easy, Exploritas provides a roommate, safe travel, and many options.” I also learned that Trafalgar Tours did the same thing. Hey, I was all set. My dream had come true! All I had to do was pack my bag and fly away. And, indeed, I did. Three months after retiring, I was on my way to Toronto, Canada, for the first of many trips. That brings us to the present. Please join me, as I reminisce.

Daphne Frutchey

Nita,
You are a dear, dear friend.
Thank you for your support.
Enjoy!
Daphne

DREAM COME TRUE

Travel with Daphne

The Best is Yet to Come

Daphne Frutchey

Dream Come True

Written by Daphne Faye Frutchey

Edited by Mary Balk

Layout, Design and Editing by Ann Zerulla

Photography and Cover by Bruce Frutchey

ISBN: 978-0-692-01169-0

E-mail: daphnef@cfl.rr.com

Printed in USA

Dedicated to my husband
Bruce, who has not only
supported my desire to travel,
but has also listened to my
stories, enhanced my photos,
and facilitated my dream so that
it could come true.

Also by Daphne Frutchey:

Middle School Trauma (2008)

ISBN: 978-1-6543210-0-0

Contents

Travel with Daphne

The Best is Yet to Come

Daphne Frutchey

Trip 1

TORONTO, CANADA

Maid of the Mist

I was beside myself with excitement as I planned my first trip since retirement. This adventure had to be a new destination and a new opportunity to learn and experience. I decided that Niagara Falls, one of the world's greatest waterfalls, would be my first stop; so I scheduled a Gray Line tour on the Canadian side of the border. It is interesting that the Niagara River flows calmly northward from Lake Erie then hastens along more swiftly as it approaches the mighty Niagara Falls. After leaping from the overhanging shelf of rock at the crest of the falls in a thunderous roar, it then seethes and churns through a narrow gorge until it suddenly spills into Lake Ontario. The river drops 315 feet in its brief length. The falls themselves drop half that distance, pouring nearly half a million tons of water in their basin every minute.

In retrospect, I would not have booked my inexpensive room in a downtown Toronto hotel. The location and price were right, but there was a big problem. I could overlook the size and lack of decor of the room because I would only be there for two nights, but I hated to share a bathroom with strangers. As I peered down the hall, I heard loud noises and laughing, causing my active imagination to take over. Of course, my idea of limiting my use of the restroom backfired. I made a plan that included a good book, barricading my door, and munching on trail mix. When I finally recalled reading that Toronto was one of the safest cities in North America, I dozed off into a fitful night of tossing and turning.

The sun awoke me early the next morning and I realized how foolish I had been to worry the night before. The Gray Line Bus arrived in front of my hotel on schedule for their tour that included the Floral Clock, the Skyline Buffet, and the Maid of the Mist tour boat. Just behind the falls on the Canadian side of the border, we were issued our blue raincoats and traveled by elevator to the famous Table Rock Scenic Tunnels.

We eagerly boarded the *Maid of the Mist* tour boat. The wind was blowing furiously and I had to struggle to wrap the large blue raincoat around my shivering body. I looked around and observed all of the blue raincoats with the hoods pulled down. We had lost our identity; everyone looked alike. Our group was united in the mission of readying ourselves for action. Our boat advanced closer and closer to the falls. I thought that we were going to plow through them. Indeed, we came closer to the Canadian Horseshoe Falls than I had anticipated. I was wet and wind blown, but I didn't care; that only added to the excitement. I was already anticipating the tale that I would share with my granddaughters. Looking back at the aerial view on my calendar, our boat was minute compared to the thundering, spraying falls.

The next day, I took a Trolley Tour to Queen's Quay and later went to the top floor of the world's tallest tower, the CN Tower. It was apparent that Toronto was a city of high rise buildings, second only to New York. As I ascended to the top floor of the CN Tower, I was a bit unnerved, especially, as I walked on the glass floor and looked below. What a view!

The Exploritas study of Global Warming supplied the new knowledge that I was eager to acquire. The classes were at Knox College, founded in 1884, and my room in the dorm overlooked a lovely garden. The first day we observed the Ontario Legislature in session. Each afternoon was spent in a classroom listening to a young female professor of science explain her view of our changing earth and atmosphere.

The professor began discussing Lake Tahoe, North America's largest alpine lake. I was suddenly intensely interested because my daughter-in-law Rose and I had hiked to Emerald Bay State Park and photographed the natural wonder, a glacier-carved blue and turquoise bay surrounded by granite peaks. Our professor stated that she expected the deep mixing of Lake Tahoe's water layers would become less frequent, depleting the bottom waters of oxygen, thus diminishing this unique, effervescent jewel. I had questions about the small, spring-fed lake in front of our home in Florida. Her answer was that the climatic changes were impacting lakes around the world because of our reliance on chemical pesticides and fertilizer. The consequences were taking an ecological and social toll, creating the decline of pristine lakes. When our family moved into our lakefront home, there were few weeds. Today the lake weeds are numerous, wrapping around our legs as we swim.

After dinner that evening, our group walked to the Panorama Hotel, another high-rise building, and took an elevator to the restaurant situated on the 51st floor for a beautiful view of Toronto. We saw the sunset on one side of the restaurant and the moonrise on the other.

Our group visited the Royal Ontario and Gardner Museums in the morning and Yorkville, bustling with savvy shoppers, in the evening. Osgoode Hall and Gardens were especially interesting because of their breathing wall in the Canada Life Environmental Room. Casa Loma, Toronto's majestic castle, and The Gallery of Ontario were on the next day's agenda. Indeed, I did have a folder full of facts about my first visit to Canada. A farewell gathering, with good food and music, ended my trip on the right note and left me anxious to plan my next venture.

THE BEST IS YET TO COME.......

Trip 2

ROME, ITALY

Michelangelo & Bernini

In searching for a trip abroad, I was drawn to Exploritas' description of a Trinity College Program designed to enlighten participants concerning the history, society and culture of Italy. Yes, I decided that Rome would be my next destination.

My flight on Alitalia Airline was a treat. The attendants were very liberal with their small bottles of white wine. When the airplane landed our leader ushered us onto a small bus and we began a short ride to our destination. I was not expecting a warm, sunny, November day complete with citrus trees. It was surprisingly like home. Our hotel, a converted monastery, was at the bottom of Palatine Hill near Circus Maximus. I was nervous about meeting my roommate, but that quickly subsided when we were introduced. I immediately liked Malinda's warm, exuberant personality.

ROME PAINTING

After the orientation session, our group took a neighborhood walk, locating the grocery store, tobacconist, newsstand, bakery and bus stop. Our chef and staff were dedicated to our gastronomical needs. We had four course meals for lunch and dinner and the staff expected us to finish each course. I found that I had to hold my hand over my soup bowl, so that the waiter would not give me seconds. Malinda and I faced our first decision, what wine to have with our meals. Our names were written on our bottles and served to us each evening. The staff explained that wine was cheaper than water or coke, so we decided, "When in Rome…" After dinner that evening, our group walked to Piazza Navona and enjoyed a gelato.

Our professors, graduates of various universities, began our lectures bright and early. Our study began with the definition of Italy's National Identity and an explanation that Northern Italy was wealthy and Southern Italy was poor. The professor identified twenty states and explained that language had been the key factor in dividing Italy and that television and soccer had been the uniting factors. After 313 AD Constantine converted to Christianity. The Roman Empire split in 395 AD and fell into the hands of barbarians in 476 AD. The Middle Ages proceeded with the age of transition. Nero started a fire to bring about urban renewal and blamed the Christians, who were martyred in Circus Maximus. However, by the 5th century 90 percent of Rome's population had become Christian and the Pantheon had become a church.

The Humanism/Renaissance periods of rebirth were renowned for guilds, clergy, bureaucracy, and aristocracy. This continued up to the 16th century. The Pieta, one of Michaelango's first sculptures, was commissioned for St. Peters, as well as the majestic Dome. Unlike many artists,

Michelangelo Buonarroti was acknowledged in his own lifetime as a supreme master of fine arts. His awe-inspiring Sistine Chapel frescoes proved that Michelangelo was truly a gifted artist.

St. Francis of Assisi had a marked effect on the language in Italy. Internal wars began to break out, and St. Francis was so concerned about poverty that he gave up his wealth to help the poor. He was jailed and his father repudiated his son's actions. As an educated man, St. Francis knew that books would have to be written in the language of the common man. Since Latin was the only printed language, he translated the books into Volgar, the common language. (We get vulgar from Volgar.) This was a remarkable transition; the poor people could now read. I knew that St. Francis loved animals and had written the Serenity Prayer, but I had no idea that he had given so much and achieved such remarkable goals.

On our field trips I was amazed at the numerous fish symbols that were on the doors. The first letters of the Greek words, Jesus Christ, formed the word "Fish", explaining the symbol for the Christians. It was interesting to observe the Christian buildings that had been built on top of the pagan structures. Our guide remarked that city officials were unable to construct new buildings or roads because their digs uncovered artifacts, forcing construction to halt.

Literary Roman highlights included Chaucer of *Canterbury Tales* and Martin Luther, who was excommunicated at the end of the 16th century because of his movement against the Catholics, when he declared that individuals were saved by faith alone. Richard Lassells, a Catholic priest, gave us *The Grand Tour.* Edwards Gibbons, Oxford, converted to Catholicism and returned to

Switzerland and wrote *The Fall of the Roman Empire*. Lord Byron (noted for his clubfoot) designated his profits from *Child Pilgrimage* to reform the world. I visited Keats and Shelley's house near the Spanish Steps and was reminded of Mad King George and the beheading of three men that caused Shelley to write, "We are as fragile as clay".

Baroque Art lectures pointed out that urbanism carved out urban zones, giving Rome its beauty, by making fountains mandatory. Nepotism promoted large palaces, as Popes installed nephews as Cardinals, namely, Prince Borghese.

Art is my passion; therefore, I capitalized phrases that are important to me. The art lecture emphasized three achievements:

1. CLARITY, INTELLIGIBILITY, AND SIMPLICITY

A great example is The *Calling of Saint Mathew* by Michelangelo Caravaggio at the Church of San Luigi dei Francesi. Mathew, the tax collector, could not believe that Jesus was calling him. Utterly surprised, Mathew pointed to himself, as if to say, "Who, me?" The particular power of the painting is the cessation of action and the indecision before reaction.

2. REACHING OUT AND GREETING THE VIEWER WITH EMOTIONAL STIMULI

The book on the desk and the chair appeared to be three-dimensional and spatial, in Caravaggio's painting, *Saint Mathew and the Angel* at the Church of San Luigi dei Francesi. A single light source created drama and reached out. Carravaggio employed Rembrandts' technique of chiaroscuro, the use of light and dark to create emotion and focus.

3. REALISTIC AND CONVINCING INTERPRETATION

In my Bible Study Fellowship classes I had learned about Peter's crucifixion. I knew that when he was placed on the cross, he requested that he be upside down so that he would not mimic his Savior's crucifixion. *The Crucifixion of Saint Peter* by Caravaggio in Cerasi Chapel, Santa Maria del Popola, was so realistic because of the lights and darks and perfection in the contours of the body that it brought tears to my eyes. When you look at St. Peter on the cross, Caravaggio places you among the sinners.

Caravaggio was born Michelangelo Merisi in 1573, in Caravaggio, Italy. As an adult he became known by the name of his birthplace. Orphaned at age 11, he was apprenticed to the painter Simone Peterzano of Milan for four years. Then Caravaggio went to Rome and worked as an assistant and began selling his paintings. Cardinal Francesco commissioned Caravaggio to paint for the church of San Luigi dei Francesi. I viewed the paintings that Caravaggio had painted for this very church in the 1500s. His works caused public outcry because of their realistic and dramatic nature. Caravaggio had many encounters with the law. Misfortune and illness overtook him and he died at the age of 27.

Contemporary Italian Society boasted that their national pastime was conversation. Fourteen languages and thirteen dialects of Italian were spoken in Italy. The year 1954 introduced national television and a national language. Without tax, lottery was the biggest source of income. The average age of marriage was 28 for women and 31 for men. Families spent approximately one and one-half hours sitting around the table eating and talking in the evening. Italy had a low birth rate and paternity was a life long responsibility. Because mortgages required a 50 percent down payment, parents assisted their children. In 1970, married couples had to wait for five years for a divorce because of church restrictions.

Contemporary Italian politics revealed that the real power of government was in the Executive and Legislative Parliament. There were 630 articles in the Italian Constitution. Power was not abused because of the multi-party representation. In the national regional, there were twenty-three political parties. There were so many parties that a Party of Love, begun by an eighteen year-old porn star, ran and won. She was actually successful because she promoted the use of condoms. The Italian Communist was the second biggest party until the Cold War was over in 1991 which brought about the Democratic Party that stood for country, family, and freedom. Italy had 56 post war governments and all of them were unstable and short term.

THE CRUCIFIXION OF SAINT PETER

There were thousands of heroin addicts and Government had not been able to control the problem. There was talk of giving free heroin to addicts who joined the health care system in order to destroy the Mafia's control. Another health issue in the community caused by needle sharing was the spread of Aids.

Ancient Roman Art surveyed the development and architecture from early Republican to late Imperial Rome. A field trip to the Roman Forum revealed sites that were a confusing patchwork of ruined buildings, temples and basilicas. Our local professor pointed out details that I would have missed, such as the indentations in the steps that were used to gamble for garments of men who had died on the cross. Soldiers tossed their pebbles onto the steps and the soldier who got most of his pebbles in the holes won the garments. John 19:24 states, "They divided my garments among them and cast lots for my clothing."

We continued on to Circus Maximus and recalled Ben Hur's chariot races in 600 BC. We gazed at the Victor Emmanuel building, built in austere white Brescian marble. The "typewriter" (an insulting nickname given to this unloved white elephant) would never mellow into the ocher tones of surrounding buildings. It was widely held to be the epitome of self-important insensitive architecture.

Our next field trip was to Santiago De Compostella to see the relics of St. James. Their cross was explained with three words. The Apse (top) was the head of the church where God was located. The transpect (cross) were the arms held out to welcome new member and the trunk (bottom) was the vassal. Our presenter drew a pyramid to represent Feudalism. From bottom to top, there were vassals, artisans, knights, nobility, clergy, and the small peak at the top, represented the King and the court.

Our day tours included the following: The Vatican, a center of power for Catholics all over the world and a sovereign state ruled by the Pope, that housed about 1000 people. Artworks covered every surface in a Vatican reception room. The 14 Vatican museums housed one of the worlds most important art collections, the Sistine Chapel and the Raphael Rooms. The massive Holy Door was only opened at the beginning, and closed at the end, of each Holy Year. Not to be missed was the helicoidal staircase designed by Michelangelo. St Peter's Basilica's vast marble-encrusted interior contained 11 chapels and 45 altars. Here we viewed Bernini's Baroque sculpture of the *Throne of St. Peter in Glory* and his famous canopy covering the papal altar. Ralph Waldo Emerson said, "I love St. Peter's Church. It is an ornament of the Earth."

Another excursion was to the Villa d'Este, whose fame rests on its terraced gardens and 100 fountains. We also toured Ostia Antica, Rome's main commercial port and military base defending the coastline and the mouth of the Tiber. Buried for centuries by sand, the city was remarkably preserved. There were 18 temples, a Jewish synagogue, and a Christian basilica

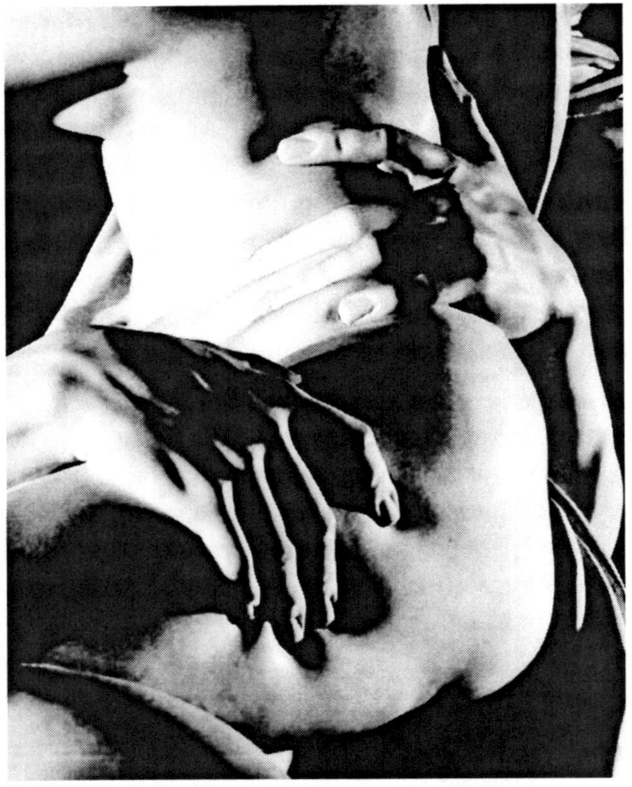

Baroque art of Rome included the paintings, sculptures and architecture of the Baroque period with a focus on the achievements of Bernini. Gian Lorenzo Bernini, the favorite artist of the Papacy, transformed Rome with his churches, palaces, statues, and fountains. On our Baroque walk, we entered the Santa Maria della Vittoria, an intimate Baroque church with a lavishly decorated candlelit interior, captaining Bernini's most ambitious sculptural works the *Ecstasy of Saint Teresa.* The sculpture, framed and illuminated by rays of divine light, evoked my deepest emotions as I fixed my eyes on the tender angel with the arrow.

Malinda and I visited the Galleria Borghese that contained Bernini's most famous works. *Pluto and Persephone* portrayed Pluto carrying off his bride. Bernini's astonishing skill with marble could be clearly seen in Pluto's imprint on Persephone's twisting body. Bernini captured David's grim determination to slay Goliath in his statue of *David.* David's jaw was set, his muscles were taunt, and he was prepared to slay the giant.

DAVID

The highlight of my trip was viewing *Daphne Fleeing the Sun God Apollo*. I was named after Bernini's most famous masterpiece and I stared in wonder at the sculpture. It came to life, as Daphne's fingers and hair turned into tendrils and leaves and her toes changed into roots. Her prayer was coming true; she was changing into a laurel tree because she did not return Apollo's love. Another statue that caught the viewer's attention was Canova's *Pauline Borghese*, Napoleon's sister, who posed semi-nude portraying Venus. Once the statue was completed,

Camillo Borghese kept it locked away, even denying Canova access.

Malinda and I turned our attention to plans for the remainder of the afternoon. We decided that, even though it was raining, we would walk through Rome on the famous Via del Corso, sight seeing and shopping. After all, it was of utmost importance to return home, empty the contents of your suitcase, and rediscover your treasures.

We visited the Church of Sant'Andrea della Valle, the Palazzo Farnese and the massive fortress of Castel Sant'Angelo where the opera *Tosca* has been immortalized and firmly enshrined. One evening we welcomed a *Tosca* performer who sang for us. We also had the opportunity to view the entire video of the opera.

Another highlight was attending a chamber musical performance by young Italian musicians. The performance was held in a large palace that housed a fantastic art collection. As I looked around the room during the concert, I noticed that we were the only Americans, which made it extra special.

By the way, we saw the Seven Hills (Quirnal, Viminal, Capitoline, Aventine, Esquiline, Celian and Palatine) near the banks of the River Tiber. On our last evening, thirty fellow travelers toasted and sang happy birthday to me. And last, but not least, since I tossed a coin into Trevi Fountain, I know that I will return.

THE BEST IS YET TO COME…….

Trip 3
San Diego, California

Tijuana Drug Arrest

When my mail arrived each day, I would eagerly open the Exploritas program and spend hours pouring over each opportunity. I finally chose the Museum Program at Balboa Park in San Diego because I am an enthusiast of museums. I also wanted to travel to California. When my departure date finally arrived, my bags were packed with special ID tags dangling on the outside of my luggage so that the program leader could identify me. I was ready for my next adventure.

The Aerospace and Automotive Museums were huge. Docents were articulate and well informed and could answer all of our questions. Also included were the Timken and Mingei Museums. Both contained treasures of unusual gifts. I bought a Chinese Interior Bottle, painted by hand. Skilled artists used extremely slender sharpened bamboo sticks that had been dipped in ink and inserted into the bottle. The artist outlined and colored a design. This method originated in China over 300 years ago during the Quing Dynasty.

Behind the Scenes Tour of San Diego Zoo took us to areas that were off limits to tourists. It was amazing to observe the dietitian's expertise concerning the carefully prepared, refrigerated foods for each animal. The portions were measured, placed in separate containers, marked, and dated. Several large black boards were charted for the day's diet for each species.

Two events delighted me. The first was observing the feeding of the newborn giraffe, so wobbly on his skinny legs. The second event was watching the giant pandas. It appeared that they were communicating very well with each other, as they sat placidly chewing on their bamboo sticks. They completely ignored the long line of tourists eagerly waiting to catch a glimpse of them.

The Museum of San Diego History featured an Imax Theatre that was very informative. Spreckels Organ Society gave concerts in the outdoor pavilion every Sunday. Booths from different countries were fun to explore. A Chinese docent at the House of Pacific Relations wrote my name in Chinese.

I really wanted to cross the U.S. border into Mexico. I thought this would be a great trip to share with my book group and grandchildren. Actually, it was more than I had anticipated. The Gray Line tour included downtown San Diego, Gaslamp Quarter, Point Loma, La Jolla, and Coronado Island and Hotel.

Finally, we journeyed to Tijuana, the gateway to Mexico. There were two border crossings into Tijuana, accounting for 300,000 daily border crossings. It was a lengthy process with cars lined up for miles. When we entered Mexico, it appeared that building codes did not exist. Shacks were roughly hammered together as far as the eye could see, many without an outside wall. As we drove up and down the hills, we observed residents' belongings; furniture, and lives were exposed. Garish nude statues were randomly placed in the oddest locations. The bus parked in the middle of town so that we could explore and enjoy lunch. On some of the street corners I noticed that donkeys were painted like zebras. I thought that it was an odd way to try to make money. However, many tourists were gathered around waiting for their turn to pose beside the donkey.

It was difficult to navigate the streets because the shops displayed mounds of merchandise piled up in front of their store windows. Merchants were loud and aggressive, pressing to make a sale. Beggars, even children, held their hands out for money. There was an overwhelming cacophony of noise and motion. I was inundated with bright, clashing colors. Even the sense of touch was different because of their roughly sewn items.

As if this were not enough, there was an open drug arrest in front of our restaurant. Guns were fired, everyone was yelling, men were pushed against the police car, searched and handcuffed. During lunch our bus driver explained that the Mexican army and police were confronted with drug cartels that resembled small combat units, with automatic weapons and grenades. After lunch, reentering this strange scene, I stuck like glue to my group, avoiding side streets. My craving for adventure was more than satisfied, and I happily climbed onto the bus and sank into my seat, breathing a sigh of relief as we crossed the porous Mexican border and returned to the United States.

THE BEST IS YET TO COME…….

Trip 4
Nashville, Tennessee

Nashville Music Industry

I was so delighted to arrive in Nashville because I had two opportunities awaiting me. One was to help my son, Bob, and future wife, Lisa, locate a restaurant for their wedding rehearsal dinner. The other was to explore Nashville.

My Southwestern flight landed on time and our Exploritas group was escorted to our dorms at Belmont University. The rooms were dreary, poorly furnished, and needed fresh paint. What a disappointment.

Thank goodness I had relatives in Nashville. After looking over my room, my son and his fiancé shook their heads and mentally took notes concerning my room makeover. The next morning, they arrived on campus with lamps, rugs, pictures, comforters, pillows, and what ever they could think of to make my stay "homey".

One of my studies was the Nashville Music Industry. Don Cusic, author, columnist, and singer, was the presenter. We listened to the Jazz Ensemble in the Bell Tower patio area and visited a studio where Nashville performers make their recordings. Imagine my delight to learn that our group would make a recording. We rehearsed Rocky Top daily until we were ready for our recording session. Each participant received a copy, and guess what, the Nashville Music Industry has nothing to worry about. Lisa's comment was "What a hoot!"

We also studied Southern & Tennessee literature. Most of our time was spent on field trips. We toured Freeman

Hall, Belmont Mansion, Opryland Hotel, The Hermitage, Tennessee State Capitol and State Museum. As we passed Vanderbilt, our guide remarked, "Vanderbilt is the intellectual oasis in a city of ignorance". His comment about Nashville was, "Nashville is the Vatican City for the Protestant religions, with over 700 churches". The trivia that I learned on this trip was that Nashville has the loudest cicadas that I had ever heard. This large insect with the ability to make such a strange noise only visits Nashville every thirteen years and my visit was very timely.

THE BEST IS YET TO COME…….

Trip 5
CHARLESTON, SOUTH CAROLINA

Secrets of Charleston

My next trip was to the College of Charleston, with its landscaped grounds and moss draped trees, dating back to the 18th century. I stayed at the Westin Francis Marion Hotel, listed in the National Register of Historic Places, and within walking distance of the College. I experienced the grace of Charleston's homes and public buildings, which embodied the colonial and antebellum spirit. The horse-drawn carriages and enviable style of living certainly seduced me. My roommate was equally exuberant about exploring this great city.

In our first lecture, I learned that Charleston (Charles Town) was named after King Charles. The first period of South Carolina history in 1497-1669 was Establishing European Claims. Then in 1670-1719 there were Proprietary Settlements and pirating. Edgar Allen Poe joined the army and wrote *Goldbug*, revealing stories about Charleston's treasures. The British Royal Colony introduced African laborers in the 1700s and the Revolution occurred in 1776. Eli Whitney and Cathy Green co-invented the Cotton Gin. Charleston was incorporated into a city in 1783. Secession, war, and a segregated state occurred in the 1800s, and Lincoln was the nominee for President in 1860.

Our architectural lectures and walks revealed a graceful, tainted, eccentric, and enduring Charleston. We observed the Colonial Style single house and Plantation house. The Georgian Style at Rainbow Row was the double house with four rooms on each level. The Federal Style displayed decorative ornament and geometric rooms. The Italianate boasted round headed arches and the Victorian contained multi-gabled roofs, turrets, and elaborate wood bracket work.

The National Russell House is noted for its free-flying elliptical staircase. The Joseph Manigault House has a marvelous history dating back to 1803. The style was Federal and the architect was Scottish. The Calhoun Mansion, George Rodgers House, Rhett House, and State House were outstanding, as was the Palladium Building where the Grand Ball was held for George Washington. Not to be missed are the US Customhouse, High Battery, The Citadel Building, and Dock Street Theatre.

Who could guess that the Council Chamber of City Hall would reveal such an interesting story? This beautiful room was the second oldest working City Council Chamber in continual use in the United States. Members of council sat at desks locally made in 1819, surrounded by original portraits of four United States Presidents and other prominent historic figures. But, as an artist, I found the following tidbit most entertaining. John Turnbul's portrait of President Washington was painted for the City of Charleston after Washington's 1791 visit. It hangs today in the historic City Hall Council Chamber. It is a great likeness of the President and the behind of his horse. Turnbul's first painting, showing the President and the head of his horse, was not only rejected but payment to the artist was refused and a demand was forthcoming for another painting. Indeed, Turnbul's first painting hangs in the University Art Gallery in the State of Connecticut and is stunning.

The churches that I especially enjoyed were the Unitarian, Circular Congregation, and St Michael's. I learned fascinating facts about St Michael's Church, 14 Street St. Michael's Alley. The large, long double-pew in the center of the church, No. 43, originally known as "The Governor's Pew was the one in which President George Washington worshipped on Sunday afternoon, May 8, 1791. General Robert E. Lee also worshipped in this pew some seventy years later. The chandelier, ordered from London in 1803, now electrified, was first lighted with candles and later with gas.

I am saving the best for last. The clock and ring of eight bells in St. Michael's Church were imported from England in 1764 and taken back to England after the Revolution as a prize of war. They were bought by a London merchant and shipped back to Charleston. When they arrived at the dock, the townspeople, overjoyed to see them again, swarmed on board ship, dragged them away, up into the steeple, and hung them immediately. Later, two bells cracked and were sent back to England to be recast. During the War Between the States the bells were sent to Columbia and were burned in the great fire there. The metal was salvaged, sent to England, and again recast by the original founders in the original molds. In 1993, the bells were refurbished and hung by Whitechapel, the original founders.

Our next lecture was titled "The Changing South" and explored topics about the New Deal Program, World War II awareness, urbanization, environmental regulations, and segregation. Our professor stated that some things had not changed, such as fifty-percent of the local population are Baptists, as well as localism and violence. A Charleston police officer discussed the homeless situation.

One evening we relived the Gullah experience, learning the song "Steal Away" accompanied by the Charleston handclap. The African rhythm taught a child that unfortunate things happen to you but Nanny is there to help and you must be patient. The speaker emphasized that harvesting, flailing, and grinding rice were daily activities.

Our next venture was Middleton Place, America's Oldest Landscaped Gardens, laid out in 1755. There was a guided tour of the house, gardens, museum, and stable. There were many varieties of azaleas and camellias in full bloom. The area was huge with ancient trees, many animals, and a blacksmith, gardener, and sculpture at work. We enjoyed our leisurely lunch with a view of the swans and cranes in the pond.

I knew that I would return to Charleston many times because of its unique appeal, its setting on a peninsula where the Ashley and Cooper rivers meet, its gardens hidden behind their wrought iron gates, and because of its hedonistic past.

MIDDLETON PLACE PAINTING

THE BEST IS YET TO COME.......

Trip 6
Vancouver/Victoria

Tragic life of famous architect

When I decided to travel to Victoria, I knew that I wanted to see Vancouver also, so I scheduled a Gray Line tour titled, "Sea Two Cities". My trip began with a grand tour of Vancouver, highlighting Stanley Park and Vancouver Art Gallery, featuring Emily Carr's totem poles and village scapes of the First Nations villages along the coast of British Columbia. My visit to Gastown was interesting because of the many artists trying to capture the eccentricity of the city on canvas. I ventured out on my own, walking through a lovely park. Suddenly, my heart sank down to my toes, as I realized my precarious situation. Homeless men, seemingly waiting for an unwary, innocent tourist, occupied the park. I looked several feet ahead and spotted two people in our group coming my way. As I ran toward them, a vagrant stepped back behind a tree. I think that I was unwittingly setting myself up. Thus my resolve to never explore alone.

Early the next morning I was on board a ferry plowing through the Gulf Islands. As we approached, I could see why Victoria was named the flower capital of Canada. Our first stop was Buchart Gardens where we viewed their spectacular floral displays. Then we enjoyed a scenic drive through the University of Victoria, the Royal Victoria Yacht Club, and Beacon Hill Park. The tour of the capital city also included the world-famous Empress Hotel, Parliament Buildings, and the Royal British Columbia Museum.

In the evening, I made my way to St Michael's University, an exclusive private boarding school, where I studied Buchart and other gardens, historic castles and artists of Victoria. St Michael's campus included lovely grounds, flowers, and charming rooms with amenities. The marvelous meals were fresh, especially the salmon.

We visited Emily Carr's home where she had kept chairs attached to the ceiling, exclaiming, "I hate a cluttered room". Emily was a writer and painter who portrayed nature in a powerful style of her own. My favorite book by Emily was *The Book of Small* on her childhood in Victoria.

The Royal Roads University and Hatley Castle were set in manicured grounds filled with Virginia Creeper, English Ivy and Wisteria vines. I especially enjoyed the statues that depicted the different seasons.

I was quite taken by the architect, Frances Rattenbury, who helped shape the landscape of Western Canada with buildings that became icons – The BC Legislature, The Empress Hotel, The Vancouver Art Gallery, and the Crystal Gardens. It was tragic that Rattenbury ended up a forgotten and ignored old man, whose only claim to fame was his murder at the hands of an eighteen-year-old servant; a servant who had been having an affair with his wife.

Rattenbury arrived in Vancouver from Yorkshire, England, in 1894, just in time to enter an architectural competition for the new BC Legislature building. He got the job but went over the budget by 100 percent. However, no one seemed to mind because the building was so spectacular.

Rattenbury also designed the inner harbor of Victoria. At this time he fell in love with Alma Packenham, ignoring the fact that he had been married forty-five years to someone else and had two grown children about the same age as Alma. When his wife refused to grant a divorce, Rattenbury moved Alma downstairs while his wife was upstairs.

His wife finally admitted defeat, but it was a hollow victory because Victoria's townspeople did not accept Alma. Rattenbury took Alma and their infant son to England and hired a local boy to help with driving and chores. Soon the boy and Alma were having an affair. In 1935 Rattenbury was murdered as he sat in his living room chair. Both Alma and George were charged with the murder; Alma was found innocent and George was found guilty. Alma committed suicide and George was later released.

Award-winning restoration work on the Parliament Buildings in 1973 and 1983 brought to completion some of the work that Rattenbury, for lack of funds, had left undone. In restoring the upper memorial rotunda and the center of the second floor, craftsmen applied some 46 ounces of 23-karat gold to the detail work.

So, when you gaze up at these architectural wonders, you may wonder how they materialized with all of the complex personality disorders that haunted Rattenbury.

THE BEST IS YET TO COME.......

Trip 7
Jerusalem, Israel

Personal Pilgrimage/15 Minutes of Fame

The number one trip of my lifetime was an International Cultural Tour detailing The Ministry of Jesus in Galilee and New Testament Jerusalem. A few weeks before my date of departure, I received an exciting letter from The Visionaries, PBS producers, stating that they were producing a documentary program about Exploritas and that their production crew would be filming in Israel during my visit. It was with great anticipation that I signed and mailed a release form to them so that I could be included in the documentary. I thought that this might be my opportunity to have "15 minutes of fame" as artist Andy Warhol put it.

The trip was a killer for many reasons. After landing at JFK in New York, I chose to walk, instead of taking the shuttle to my departure gate. This was a bad choice because I had two suitcases in tow in 22-degree weather. When I finally reached El Al Airlines, their doors were locked! After a few desperate minutes, I spotted workers slipping into the building through a side door. I followed them and walked into the business class lounge where I enjoyed hot coffee and snacks, helping me pass the time before my plane departure.

In the main lobby, I was relieved to see other Exploritas travelers. The next piece to the puzzle was to find our departure gate. We discovered that the gates were not posted until a few minutes before the flight. We were politely waiting for other flights to depart, when we realized that numbers and destinations were not being announced.

Then our flight appeared on their departing schedule and we rushed to the gate and boarded the airplane, noticing that passengers were already seated. We quickly located our seats, buckled in, and our flight lifted off the runway at 12:20 a.m.

When we arrived at Israel's Ben Gurion Airport, a representative met us. After clearing customs, we were escorted to our waiting bus for a two-hour ride to En Gev Holiday Village. I will not go into roommate details, but suffice it to say that my luck ran out. Rossi, our fantastic group leader, matched roommates again and "all's well that ends well". Many of our group members were in the medical field, dedicated to learning, taking copious notes, and asking many questions. We all had difficulties keeping up with the oldest member, a 91-year-old gentleman.

We finally settled into our guestrooms and I gazed out of my window. I could see the lights of Tiberias twinkling across the lake. I thought back to my studies recalling that Galilee was originally home to the Cananites, then to David and to Solomon, and in the 8th century BC to the Assyrians. In the Middle Ages the city of Safed in upper Galilee was a center of mysticism known as the Kabbala.

In the emotionally charged setting of the Holy Land, Judaism and Islam played an important part in this crossroads of Christianity. The Holy Land was the setting for the life, preaching, miracles, and sacrifice of Jesus. The sites associated with Jesus – the visible signs of an extraordinary past, the vast archaeological remains, the turmoil of faith and the Holy Places – invited us to deep reflection. I learned that a visit to Israel becomes a pilgrimage.

You cannot remain indifferent when you are participating in communion in a local church, strolling through the

Garden of Gethsemane, and walking in Jesus' footsteps along the Via Dolorosa.

SEA OF GALILEE - PAINTING

Our first study tour took us to Nain, a small town at the foothills of Mt. Tabor, where Jesus met a widow standing beside the dead body of her only son. Jesus felt compassion for the widow and brought her son back to life, as the crowd watched in jubilation (Luke 7:11-16). Mt. Tabor was identified as the Transfiguration Mountain where Jesus was given a special role next to the two pivotal characters, Moses and Elijah, who symbolized Law and Order. Peter, James and John, Jesus' disciples, witnessed Jesus' transfiguration (Mathew 17:1-9).

Our next stop was Megiddo, one of the most ancient cities in the land of Israel, first settled about six thousand years ago. Throughout history, Megiddo had been a large and significant city, governed by many sovereigns such the King Thut-Mose, King Solomon and King Ahab. Its strategic character found expression in Christian tradition, because Megiddo is the Armageddon in which the final battle between Good and Evil will be fought at the "End of the Days" (Revelation 16:12-16).

Continuing our study tour, we visited Nazareth where the Angel Gabriel revealed to Mary that she was to give birth to a son who was destined to become grand and superior (Luke 1:26-38). Mary's son, Jesus, was brought up and educated in Nazareth. We stopped in Cana, the place where Jesus turned the water into wine at a wedding feast of the poor (John 2:1-11). This was the first reported miracle of Jesus. Tradition saw in this event the model for the first Christian wedding and family.

We visited several National Parks, such as Hamat Tiberias, Korzim, and Caesarea. We observed pilgrims being baptized in Jordan's holy water at Yardenit, the charming baptismal site on the Jordan River bank. As we sailed back to En Gev across the Sea of Galilee, I was reminded of the biblical story of Jesus calming the storm.

After crossing the sea, we journeyed to Tabgha where Jesus miraculously multiplied two fish and five loaves of bread to feed the hungry multitudes that followed him (John 21:15-17). That evening at dinner in a local restaurant, I ordered St. Peter's fish – a real treat – fins, head, eyes and all!

We had a guest speaker one evening, a young woman who lived in the Ein Gev Kibbutz. She stated that all earnings, such as her husband's twelve-hour a day paycheck, went into a central fund. Her grandfather, who had been imprisoned in a concentration camp, still worked part-time. Her 17-year-old son was scheduled to go into the military the next year for three years. Since everyone worked, there was a communal childcare center. There was also a special building for the care of the infirm and elderly. Living quarters were tiny because of the communal dining and laundry facilities. She stated that there was a total absence of need or desire for possessions. We toured the outside of this kibbutz and it was dirty, dismal and dreary. I could not imagine living in those conditions.

As our bus neared the Golan Heights, we could see the barbed wire fences, towers, and army trucks. Suddenly, Rossi announced that we had to take a detour because the bridge that we had planned to cross had been blown up. I said a silent prayer thanking God that I lived in the United States.

We were near Jerusalem when I noticed that all traffic had stopped and that there were several policemen, armed with riffles, searching the cars. Rossi told us that, if an unidentified bag was reported, traffic stopped and searches continued until the bag was found. In about an hour, we were assured that all was well and that there was no bomb. Soldiers stationed at each door searched our bags and purses as we checked in the Mercure Jerusalem Gate Hotel. On a lighter note, we were advised to take elevator #1 because we could operate it. The other elevators would automatically stop at every floor because the Jews did not push any buttons on their Sabbath. The next morning our breakfast was cold boiled eggs, a salad bar, and coffee in a huge thermos. The hotel was very quiet because there was no traffic and stores were closed.

Jerusalem was a city that defined diversity with its interaction, cooperation, and conflict between old and new, East and West, the secular and the religious. For millions, Jerusalem was the soul of the Universe. I was continuing my pilgrimage and ready for the next exciting development. Indeed, it had begun. The production crew associated with the Visionaries, who would be producing the documentary during our week in Jerusalem, had arrived. They would be filming us as we listened to lectures and toured the great, busy city. At first, I was distracted and excited because I wanted to observe their technique and talk to the young crew. Then, I settled down and we departed for Ein Kerem, the birthplace of John the Baptist, and home of the Biblical Resources Study Center that served the Jews, Christians and Muslims.

The Center was a serene oasis with a bookstore, courtyard, and roof garden. We enjoyed our lunches on the roof and our picturesque view of the hillside village. In the courtyard, there were replicas of Bedouin tents containing cooking utensils, complete with a water well nearby. (We drove past tents like these on our way to Jerusalem.) There were crosses near the same area, similar to those used during the lifetime of Jesus. Some were constructed crosses, but most were trees with horizontal boards for outstretched arms and for the feet. I shuddered as I stared at these crude crosses. Dwellings made of stones were in the courtyard, as well as tombs, complete with the large stone that could be rolled away in order to enter the tomb.

I was surprised to learn that there were many different types of colleges in Jerusalem, including a large Mormon University. The prerequisite for attendance was a signed statement that there would be no proselytizing.

Our afternoon field trip took us to Bethlehem, the place where Joseph and Mary came to register as ordered by the Emperor Augustus (Matthew 1:18-25). We saw the Basilica of the Nativity with the Silver Star, lit by fifteen lamps, marking the exact point where Jesus was born. In 135 AD the Emperor Hadrian, in his effort to eradicate the Christian religion, dedicated the grotto to the pagan god Adonis. Not until the intervention of Constantine in 332 was it possible for Christians to pray in one of the places dearest to Christian tradition. Access to the basilica was by the very small Door of Humility (four feet). We had to enter bending over, as if going into a real cave. Originally, the door must have been far larger; it was reduced in size around the seventh century, so that the Muslims could not ride into the church on their horses. In the Grotto of the same name stood The Altar of Christ's Birth and The Altar of the Manger. It was awesome, singing, "Oh Little Town of Bethlehem" in the grotto where Mary gave birth to Jesus.

The next morning we met our lecturer and tour guide, Randy Smith, who had earned several degrees, including a Ph.D. in Jewish Studies, qualifying him to be a Rabbi. Randy owned a company titled, "Christian Travel Study Programs" that encompassed five countries, including Africa and Europe. His credentials included programs in Israel and the United States (on the History Channel with International Studies) and his twenty-year residency in Jerusalem. Randy's dynamic presentations held us spellbound.

Randy's first lecture was titled, "Jesus and the Temple Mount". The differences that Randy found between the United States and Israel were as follows:

1. In Israel there was no personal space so locks had to be placed on doors so that others would not walk in.
2. In Israel everyone was in charge.
3. Time – The past was the present and Israelites still argued about events that occurred 2000 years ago.
4. Israelites preached Paul, not Jesus.

Randy's comments concerning the Middle East included the following important points:

1. In the Middle East, verbs were used to describe the function. The United States used pronouns as I, me.
2. In the Middle East, it was not rude to talk while someone else was talking. At first the Israelites thought that Randy was stupid for not talking.
3. Israelites were physically active and did not know what to do with peace. They were a wounded society with a chip on their shoulder. "Just because you stop being paranoid, doesn't mean everyone isn't out to get you." Randy stated that his children learned to push back because they were taught "never to be victimized".

The primary differences between the Christians and Jews, according to Randy, were:

1. The Christians championed forgiveness and the Jews championed remembrance.
2. The Christians believed that birthdays were important and in Israel they celebrated the "death day".
3. Christians expressed ownership and relationship.
4. Jews thought that what you did was not important. They wanted to know what God did. Also, they were not concerned about God's appearance.
5. Jews said, "You know my God by the way I behave". Young people were responsible for their parents, so parents had no need for social security. Randy said that his daughter was safe going out at night in Jerusalem.

In a discussion about the changes that are taking place during worship in the United States, Randy stated that there is confusion and theology has been boiled down to the lowest common denominator. Worship has become more charismatic and church members experience everything and know nothing. He compared it to listening in on a phone conversation, where you know the answers, but not the questions. Randy concluded, "In our pulpits, the symptoms are being treated, not the problems."

In the afternoon we departed for a study tour of the Western Wall. I learned that in 63 BC Herod the Great controlled Jerusalem. During his thirty-six year reign the city grew in wealth and Herod renovated the Temple and reinforced its court with massive supporting walls. The remnant of Herod's retaining wall was a revered and sacred site for the Jewish religion and is known today as the "Western Wall". As we approached, we could see that the area was carefully guarded. There were many Orthodox Jews dressed in their long black robes praying by the wall. We noticed that the men and women were separated, facing the wall saying their prayers and placing their written prayers in the wall. The camera crew was busy trying to encompass Randy's gestures and words, while filming our group's reaction.

As part of our cultural program, we spent the evening at the Israel Museum. The most amazing things that I saw were The Dead Sea Scrolls. A Bedouin boy accidentally discovered these ancient Hebrew scrolls in 1947 in the Judean Desert. The young shepherd was certainly unaware of destiny when his innocent search for a stray goat led to the fateful discovery of the scrolls in a long untouched cave. One discovery led to another, and eleven scrolls were eventually uncovered. The scrolls contained:

- Songs of the Sabbath Sacrifice
- Prayer for King Jonathan
- Paleo-Hebrew Leviticus Scroll
- Psalms Scroll
- Most of the books of the Bible

These scrolls existed because of the Essenes and their separatist lives through two centuries, occupying themselves with study, worship and prayer. The Dead Sea Scrolls have played a major role in improving our comprehension of this pivotal moment in Jewish history!

On our way to the Biblical Resource Study Center, Randy pointed to a boxcar on the side of the mountain that had been used by the Nazi Germans. The Jews choose to keep it there as a constant reminder. After our tour of Mt. Zion, including the Upper Room, he mentioned that Schindler was buried on the East Side of Zion.

Randy's special gift was making everything that we had learned about the Biblical characters come alive. The words jumped off the pages of the Bible in the form of a place or a person. His description of the reason that Jesus was not discovered for three days after his family's return was a good example. Randy stated that men and women traveled in separate camps and Mary thought that Jesus was with Joseph and Joseph thought that Jesus was with Mary. It took Joseph a week to go to Nazareth and bring Jesus back. Randy exclaimed that this was not a hygienic story; Joseph was worried and angry. He said, "We doom our young people because we treat these stories as unreal". Dennis, a Visionary team member, remarked, "Now I want to attend church because I can view these people as real!" (Parenthetically, Randy said that Arab women are suffering because of running water. Today they do not have their time to talk to other women by the well.)

His summation of the first four authors of the New Testament was:

1. Matthew taught words as Sermon on the Mount.
2. Mark taught works as "straight way".
3. Luke taught order as chronology.
4. John spoke of conflict.

Our morning lecture was titled, "Jesus in the Jewish and Roman Court". Saturday before Jesus arrived at Bethany in Kidron Valley (where he was anointed) Jesus was with Simon the leper, Mary, Martha the activist, and Lazarus.

The Passion Week events that occurred before Jesus' death took place were as follows:

1. Sabbath – COMPASSION – The first plot was to get rid of Lazarus, hoping that Jesus' popularity would fade.
2. Palm Sunday – POPULARITY – 250,000 people crowded into Jerusalem to see Jesus' "Triumphal Entry".
3. Monday – AUTHORITY – Cleansing of the temple which created anger and attention.
4. Tuesday – TESTING – JESUS IN THE ROMAN COURTS – temple – court examinations.
5. Wednesday – SILENCE – Fast of the firstborn.
6. Thursday – DESPAIR – Meal in the upper room where the disciples argued as to where they would sit. There was washing of the feet as Jesus said, "Love one another as I have loved you." There was the prayer in Gethsemane, where Jesus told the disciples, "I am going away and I am going to return." There was betrayal and arrest. Jesus went before Annas Caiphas, and Peter denied knowing Jesus three times.
7. Friday – VIOLENCE – Judas betrayed Jesus. Jesus went before Herod Antipas and Pilate, who sentenced Jesus to be crucified. Jesus prayed, "Father let this cup…"Pilate could not find any fault with Jesus and ordered that Jesus be whipped 39 – not 40 times (beat within an

> inch of his life). Glass, metal, and bone chips were in the whip that destroyed the bone structure of Jesus' back. Two thieves hung on either side of Jesus. One believed and Jesus said, "This day you will be in Paradise". One did not believe and all human history is divided in this way.

The Temple veil was rent, Jesus' side was pierced, and he was removed from the cross. His body was rubbed with spices and oils to break it down faster. Jesus was in the tomb three days and nights. JESUS APPEARED MANY TIMES AFTER HIS RESURRECTION.

Randy said that Civil and Religious Courts still exist in Arabia and Africa. The UN had 40 Arabs and one Jewish representative. Female circumcision still exists and is horrible, causing many infections.

Our tour of Jerusalem included many sights, including the Aqsa Mosque, Dome of the Rock, and the Chagall Windows in the Medical Center. The Jewish Quarters were an intricate maze with the fascinating, close knit intimacy of a village. One loses all sense of direction as you weave in and out of the passageways. The allure of spices and the pungent aroma of warm Arabic bread filled our nostrils. We suddenly came upon a sign that read, "You have descended three meters below the level of the present Jewish Quarter. You have gone back two thousand years in time, to the Upper City of Jerusalem in the Herodian Period."

I was surprised that our group had so quickly accepted the camera crew as part of our entourage. While filming, the crew made discoveries and learned along with us. Because I had been asked to participate in the interview, I had difficulty falling asleep that evening thinking about what I would say the next morning. When my breathing became shallow I knew that I was making too much “ado” about this situation. So I did what I normally do when I am stressed; I prayed and asked God for peace. God answered my prayer and I slept well.

The young crew was helpful, prepping me for the camera and my interview. I had completed my personal pilgrimage, following in Jesus’ footsteps through the Holy Land, and had felt Jesus’ presence as I progressed from the “fairy tale” approach of Bible study to the “hands on” reality. The filming session went well and now I could relax and enjoy our Last Supper, a Biblical Meal with a unique atmosphere, authentic food, and enlightening discussion of the events, which took place 2000 years ago.

GARDEN OF GETHSEMANE - PAINTING

After returning home, a friend nonchalantly remarked, "I saw you on TV when I was vacationing in California". After recovering from my shock, I telephoned The Visionaries and was able to purchase two videos of their Adventures in Traveling, narrated by Sam Waterson. His theme was "shattering negative stereotypes concerning ageism". He maintained that people in a certain age bracket were treated in a different way because of prejudice against older adults. The first trek that The Visionaries and Exploritas took was the Jungle Safari in Nepal. Israel was the second pilgrimage. Sam also covered the Intergenerational Program entitled, "Fly, Fly, Fly" at Embry Riddle Aeronautical University and the Mentoring Program on the Navaho Reservation.

Sam Waterson's closing quote was "Grow old along with me, the best is yet to be, the last of life for which the first was made." Robert Browning.

THE BEST IS YET TO COME…….

Trip 8
Spain & Portugal

Dali and Gaudi

Travel is not only fun; it also gives you a sense of freedom and adventure. Exploring other countries promotes understanding and appreciation of different cultures, while broadening your perspective and changing your views. The sweeping mosaic of creativity expressed in the art and architecture of Spain and Portugal contributed to the transformation of modern Europe.

After signing up for a 21-day tour, I was destined to experience the diversity and intensity of these countries.

The beginning of my trip was frustrating because of the two-day delay resulting from snowstorms in New York, my departure city. Throughout the entire trip, I wore a special vest that concealed my documents and money. I had been warned about thieves and I did not want to be a victim. (I also placed my documents in the room safes at each stop.) I made an unpleasant discovery concerning the heating in the hotel rooms; turning up the thermostat did not change the temperature. I finally found the solution – sleeping in several warm outfits, topped by a blanket and my winter coat. It alarmed me when I learned that my keycard must be inserted in the television and wall switches to access each service. I did not mind placing the keycard in the elevator slot, but it was a little frightening to have to insert the key in a slot every few feet as I walked down the long, dark hallway to my room.

Our arrival city, Lisbon, was inhabited at least 2500 years before the birth of Christ. Its renowned harbor became the entryway for enormous wealth from New Worlds. The Monument to the Discoveries, a tribute to the brave Portuguese who took part in the ocean crossings in the 15th century, and the fortress, Bethlehem Tower, portrayed a difficult time in their history. Our last evening in Lisbon was an introduction to the Portuguese Fado, sad, mournful ballads accompanied by a mandolin.

Our next city was Coimbra, one of the major European cultural centers. I was fortunate to have this wonderful opportunity to visit ancient cities, so rich in culture and beauty. Centuries of history lay under a fine mantle of whitewashed houses, intersected by winding streets, steps and arches and the majesty of monuments. In 1290, the King decreed the Royal Charter to build the University. This singular institution contained the King John Library, a home to the bats that ate the bothersome insects.

Oporto, our wine stop, housed the great Sandeman Porto Cellar and Caves of Port Wine. A young woman dressed in black, with a black cape and hat, dramatically swung open the door for our group. She escorted us to the wine cellar for tasting, relaxing, and snacking. On the way back to the bus, I noticed laundry hanging out to dry. I asked Colin, our guide, about this and he informed me that there were few washers and dryers in Portugal. We visited Viana Do Castelo in Braga and saw the artwork that displayed an extravagant, touching portrayal of Christ's death at the altar.

When we crossed into Spain, the terrain changed from rocks and hills to flat, green landscapes filled with oak trees and storks. Colin advised us not to attend the cruel, gory bullfights. Our first stop, Salamanca, the "Golden City", sat 2,450 feet above sea level beside the river Tormes and was the first city to have its own university in 1220. I would be remiss if I did not mention our great food. Conversations were sparkling due to our many Ph.D. travelers. Among them were a minister, Lt. Colonel, architect, and a life master's duplicate bridge player.

The next day, we arrived in Madrid, the "European capital of Arts". Madrid became the Golden Age's tremendously wealthy and powerful city during the Habsburg monarchy in the 16th century. The many architectural styles were Austrian, Baroque, Courtly and Classic.

The Prado Museum (home of *The Maids of Honour* by Velaquez and Rubens, *The Three Graces*), Thyssen Bornemisza Collection and Reina Sofia Arts Center were magnificent. I could not take my eyes off Picasso's shocking *Guernica* (a small town) because his huge composition reflected total chaos. There were symbols of disaster such as an anguished mother with a dead child, a wounded horse representing the Spanish people, a crucifixion gesture, and witnesses staring in disbelief. *Guernica* depicted Europe's first air raid on civilians in 1937.

It was such a treat to see the actual paintings that I had admired in my art books. I observed the details of thick paint applied in some areas and soft rendering in others. After leaving the museum, I strolled down the street and decided to pop into a café. Imagine my surprise to look up at the walls in the café and see bulls staring back at me. Apparently, taxidermists have a thriving business in Spain.

The magnificent Royal Palace of Madrid, with its ceiling frescos, Main Vestibule and staircases, paintings, Porcelain, Billiard and Gala Dining Rooms, Royal Chapel and Library were ultra opulent. The Palace was a labyrinth composed of three stories underground and five above ground. The Main

Courtyard, Royal Armory and Pharmacy were outstanding, as was the Fountain of the Shells.

We took a field trip to Toledo, home of Don Quixote, to see Elgreco's Museum Masterpiece at Santo Tome. Indeed, El Greco's *Burial of the Conde de Orgaz* was exceptional. I thought of Jerusalem as we made our way through the tangle of steep, narrow, higgledy-piggledy streets forming a veritable maze. Around every corner, we would stumble into churches, monasteries, or religious schools. Toledo smacked of fortitude, melancholy, and mysticism, just as El Greco painted it. The age-old city boasted of having three cultures – Christian, Arab and Hebrew.

As I entered the Toledo Cathedral, I had the same overwhelming feeling that engulfed me at St Peter's Basilica. Its architecture reflected the Spanish Gothic art since it took over two hundred years to build, from 1227 to 1493. The splendor of Toledo's massive cathedral reflected its history as the spiritual heart of the Spanish church. El Greco's The *Denuding of Christ*, above the marble altar was painted especially for the cathedral. The 10-foot high monstrance was carried through the streets during the Corpus Christi celebrations. The chapter house, high altar and choir were remarkable. The ornate skylight illuminated the *transparente*, a Baroque altarpiece of marble, jasper and bronze.

On the trip back to Barcelona, our guide, Colin, told great jokes, warning us that a cold in Spanish was *constapato*. He declared that "I put me heart and soul into this job", and he really did. He was energetic, running early every morning before his busy day with us. He required only a few hours of sleep. Colin revealed that he was a vegetarian and had an autistic daughter. As we cut through the hills, we listened to guitar music while viewing the Pyrenees and Monseuratt.

We spent six days enjoying lectures at the National Museum of Art of Catalonia situated in Barcelona Harbor, dining in a cafe overlooking the Mediterranean. Don Quixote wrote, "Barcelona, the treasure house of courtesy, the refuge of strangers". The capital of Catalonia had been an active port and a center of economic power and cultural vitality. Barcelona's ambience attracted well-known painters, architects, artists, two World Fairs, and the Olympics.

Our lectures included Picasso, Miro, and Dali, as well as visits to their museums. Our field trip to Dali Foundation in Figueres was most exciting. As we approached the museum, I was startled to see huge eggs perched on the top of the main entrance and on the brick fence. In the courtyard, I was surprised to discover a Cadillac with a large statue of a nude woman standing on the hood. Equally dismaying, was the Mae West Room, complete with stairs and a viewing platform to observe large red lips, an object that was presumably her nose and two framed pictures of eyes above. The funny thing was that Dali successfully captured Mae West's essence.

Included in Dali's Museum was Dali painting Gala from the back eternalized by six virtual corneas provisionally reflected by six real mirrors. Our lecturer said that Dali was incredibly infatuated with Gala, who left her husband and child to be with him. Dali's *Basket of Bread* was featured in his museum. When asked to display this painting in the United States, Dali demanded two first class tickets one for himself and one for his famous masterpiece.

Our group continued to Pubol, home of Gala's Castle that Dali had built for her. Inside we stared at Gala's throne (on a raised platform), and royal chair, complete with a crown. On the third floor, we could view (behind glass) Gala's wardrobe, perfectly fitted on mannequins. The small castle and quaint town were quite charming.

Our next excursion was to Cathedral Square to join the Sandanas Dancers in the "pi" square where the local artists gathered on Sundays. It was a festive occasion with a small orchestra, smiles, greetings, and dancing. Most of us learned the dance and joined in with the locals. There was a special celebration and parade after the dance, featuring performers on stilts, dressed in period costumes. As we boarded the bus to leave, I was distressed to learn that three members of our group were the victims of thieves.

Several of us walked down Las Ramblas, the Pedestrian-friendly Boulevard, observing street performers such as human statues, artists, and strolling musicians. The boulevard was peppered with tapas bars and flower shops. The "Ramblas experience" left me giddy, with energy building in lilting stages. If you weren't already in love with stylish, sensuous, wacky Barcelona, this would seal the deal.

Our field trips included Gaudi's *Parc Guell, La Padrera & Sagrada Familia,* Barcelona's most emblematic buildings. Antoni Gaudi was at the forefront of the Art Nouveau movement in Spain. His work in Barcelona led to the creation of some of the city's most notable landmarks. Gaudi was a pioneer in his field using color, texture, and movement in ways never before imagined. His works stand as testimony to his genius. His discoveries were based on nature – on God's creation. Gaudi proclaimed, "The greatest architect is God." Standing in Gaudi's bedroom, containing only the barest necessities, such as his twin bed and chest and a simple cross and religious pictures on the wall, I was reminded of Van Gough's painting of his bedroom. In the garden that led to Gaudi's little apartment, he had designed large, marble balls along the lengthy path. Our lecturer stated that Gaudi was very religious and that he said prayers as he passed each ball, similar to the use of a rosary.

Interesting facts about Gaudi are that he never married, lived like a monk, was an introvert keeping to himself, and went to church every day. His friends were his assistants and he kept these artisans all of his life. The catenary arches, curved surfaces, and his introduction of light in the interior courtyards for ventilation were integrated in his *La Pedrera* – white ceramic topped apartment. The Padrera building portrayed the inseparability of art and technology. Our visit on the roof, observing the remarkable design of the skylights and chimneys and enjoying the view over the city, was inspiring. Our guide remarked, "The building is still shocking us."

Trencadis, the mosaic technique so notably put to use by Gaudi, was one of *Park Guells* most characteristic features. Today the Park forms the city's heritage and that of humanity, having been afforded this status by UNESCO. The huge mosaic iguana, weird slanted walkway, and snake-like seats were unforgettable.

The Sagrada Familia, under construction since 1882 and on course for completion in 2030, is to Barcelona what the Eiffel Tower is to Paris, an irreplaceable logo. In later years, Gaudi literally begged for funds, knocking on the doors of the wealthy. A streetcar killed the most famous architect that Barcelona ever produced in 1926. Wearing a threadbare black suit, his pockets empty with neither identification nor money, he was hustled away to the public ward of a hospital, where friends found him the next day.

He refused to be moved and died among the poor two days later. He did not have the opportunity to witness 10,000 mourners who followed the casket to his grave. The Vatican officially initiated the process that could make Gaudi the first architect to be brought into its Canon of Saints. There will never be another Gaudi!

All too soon, it was time to depart for Lisbon. We had a 4 am wake-up call; and, upon arriving at the airport, I discovered that my suitcase was missing. Colin immediately sent a taxi back to the hotel to retrieve my luggage. We made the best of our six-hour delay in Lisbon by playing bridge and enjoying a free three-course meal. I learned some valuable lessons – never fly T.A.P. (Take Another Plane) Airlines, never choose JFK Airport as your departure, and never, never accept a schedule that requires three flights home. Would I do it again? You bet!

After returning home, I threw a celebratory Tapas Party, delighting my guests with a dramatic Flamenco dance by Mary (a best friend) and her dance partner. We celebrated the Spanish culture highlighted by my newly acquired broad perspective and changed views!

THE BEST IS YET TO COME…….

Tour 9
Greece & Santorini

Tea in Santorini

My original search for a guide fluent in Greek and an artist who taught watercolor was successful, so I signed up for the tour. Then I received news that the Art Tour was cancelled. I decided to continue on my own, signing up for Trafalgar's "Best of Greece Tour". The plan to travel to Santorini was more difficult to devise. My travel agent recommended a Trafalgar property in Fira, Santorini. Tourlite International provided my flight from Athens, transfers, and four nights at the El Greco Hotel, complete with a buffet breakfast each morning. After finalizing my plans, I relaxed and waited.

Departure day finally arrived and my British Airways flight to London was great, partially because of an empty aisle seat next to me. The last four-hour leg of my flight to Athens "flew" by and I was greeted at the airport by a Trafalgar representative and whisked away to the Royal Olympic Hotel.

Our group sightseeing agenda began with a ride to the extraordinary 2000-year-old Acropolis. The cultural achieve-ments included the Theatre of Dionysos, the Theatre of Herodes Atticus, and the Parthenon. I found the illusion of perfection in the Parthenon interesting with its visual trickery used to counteract the laws of perspective. The Temple of Olympian Zeus, situated next to Hadrian's Arch, was the largest in Greece, exceeding even the Parthenon in size.

When planning my trip, I had no idea that I would arrive in Greece during Easter, their biggest holiday. Rouli, our guide, took special bread to the Olympic Stadium (built for the first modern Olympic Games in 1896) so that we could share and celebrate their Easter. We journeyed to the Plaka in Athens for dinner and were utterly amazed to see the archway, church, and tower lighted with white lights (like Christmas). There were hundreds of families carrying lit candles, singing and walking in a processional into the church. What a special, lovely celebration! Thus ended our first day and our group gratefully returned to our hotel. I had a surprise waiting, two red Easter eggs, special bread, and a lovely card that read, “He is Risen”. Rouli explained the next day that, “We crack eggs with another and say, He is Risen. and then we turn the egg around and crack our eggs together again and say, He is Risen, indeed.”

The next day we drove to the bridge across the Corinth Canal, a narrow isthmus used for transporting goods. We visited the Beehive Tombs, Lion Gate, and Royal Palace. We drove through the Mountains of Arcadia to Olympia, where the first Olympic Games were held in 776 BC and then on to Delphi and the Sanctuary of Apollo. As we approached ancient Delphi, the mountain streams and countryside were serene, untouched and beautiful. Rouli quoted this legend – “When Zeus released two eagles from opposite ends of the world their paths crossed in the sky above Delphi, establishing the site as the center of the Earth.” We actually observed the “Naval of the Earth”, an unusual small, rudimentary sculpture. Rouli walked with us to the Sanctuary of Apollo and the sacred spring. She related that the British romantic poet, Lord Byron, once plunged into the spring, inspired by the belief that the waters would enhance the poetic spirit.

We were up early anticipating our long trek to the incredible monasteries of Meteora, perched on precipitous rocks. The strangely varied landscapes that have few parallels anywhere in the world struck me with a curious mixture of awe and amazement. The scenery suggested a vision of the world in the first days of Creation. As we drew closer, the fog closed in like a mask on the gigantic rocks. A strange sensation gripped me as I heard the north wind whistle down the sheer rock. We kept wiping our bus windows, trying to bring the outside into focus, not being able to comprehend what we were seeing. The immense rocks threw deep, menacing shadows across the landscape, as we gazed with wonderment.

We drove past destitute hermits who had turned their backs upon the world to live in caves on huge rocks with a chasm below. Rouli remarked that they prayed night and day, beseeching God to grant their soul eternal rest; and, indeed, some had breathed their last there in isolation and oblivion.

Cresting these great rocky eminences, the monasteries seemed poised between earth and sky in their endeavor to reach closer to God in Heaven. Our first visit was to the monastery of the Metamorphosis of the Savior. In former times the ascent was by hanging ladders or a net in which visitors, baggage and supplies were hoisted up with the help of a windlass. We got a good look at this contraption and most of us remembered James Bond using it in the movie, "For Your Eyes Only". Since 1923 a short tunnel and 146 steps cut into the rock have made the ascent somewhat easier.

It seemed so strange rummaging through a large box for a skirt that I could put on over my slacks in order to enter the chapel. The sacristies and libraries of the Meteora monasteries comprised one of the richest spiritual and artistic storehouses of the Orthodox religion. They contained historic heirlooms, which have been lovingly cherished down through the centuries. The leather-bound Gospels with gold tooling, enameled crosses with precious stones, paintings too numerous to mention, and Byzantine frescoes delighted us. The monasteries were small and cozy, almost like a cocoon with the sluggish oil lamps flickering in the tiny windows of the monks' cells, sending out their faint message that there was still life in that somber void. I felt transported far from mundane things to an unearthly world filled with prayers and psalms, drawn to communicate directly with God.

The Monastery of Saint Stephen, the richest on Meteora, stood on an immense rock overlooking Kalambaka, our small town and destination for the evening. The small chapel, erected in the 15th century, was built as a basilica and contained magnificent murals.

On the way back to Athens, we stopped at a studio in which a local priest displayed his icons. He was painting when we arrived. After I purchased one of his paintings, I read my certificate on the back, "Exact copy of the strict Byzantine style created by Father Pefkis", stamped and signed by the artist. This treasure will always spark my memory of Greece. We celebrated our last evening in a local restaurant in the festive Plaka, dining, drinking, being entertained and saying goodbye to newfound friends.

SANTORINI PAINTING

The eruption of Santorini 3,600 years ago shook the world and continues to puzzle scholars today. The removal of such a large volume of magma caused the volcano to collapse, producing a caldera. The colors of the Aegean Sea, the strong light, the transparency of its horizon, the depth of the santorini blue created magnificent beauty that tended to make you forget the nightmare of its creation. Architects say that within two centuries of the eruption people were dwelling there again. The volcanic ash, one to two hundred feet in depth, was a perfect building material for lodging. People could dig a hole in the ash and paint the walls white to create a room and carve out more ash, as more rooms were needed.

My Olympic flight to Santorini was an hour late and I was dying to see the Greek islands in the daylight. We finally left at sunset and gazed in wonder at the islands illuminated by the setting sun. I actually saw the sun set twice, once before boarding the plane, then again after taking off. Our small plane was flying quite low. Coming in for a landing was a thriller. We swooped around in a 180-degree turn and from my window seat, it looked like the right wing would dip into the ocean.

The Santorini Airport was tiny and I immediately spotted Far & Wide Tours. The guide and driver picked up my luggage and pointed out important landmarks on the map and handed me a packet while driving across town to El Greco, my home away from home for four nights. What a charming, beautiful hotel and such friendly service at 9:45 p.m. from Angie and Marios, the young managers. They spoke several languages and were eager to be of assistance. I immediately enlisted their help in choosing and booking a tour, Discover Santorini, for my first day.

I was extremely pleased with my room; it exceeded my expectations. In addition to its charm, it was meticulously clean, large, and new. It had indirect light, shuttered and draped windows, a music system, built in cabinets, and a television mounted high on the wall. There was a lovely, well-lit, tiled bathroom.

The buffet breakfasts were a feast and I was able to make a nice cheese sandwich to take with me for lunch. My day was off to a good start and I thought I was ready to board my bus. When I stopped at the front desk for my vouchers, Angie asked me, "Do you have your bathing suit on"? I did not, so I had to rush into their restroom and put it on under my clothes. She asked if my important papers were secure. My answer was no, so she took them and put them in their safe. As you can see, I was nervous and not accustomed to jumping off a boat in the middle of the ocean. I felt like a first grader on my first day at school. Angie grinned and waved goodbye as I boarded my bus.

We started our tour at the Ancient City of Akrotiri, a Minoan City that was being excavated. It was a remarkable discovery with multistory houses all connected by a sophisticated central drainage system. Each house appeared to have been inhabited by wealthy families and had at least one room lined with frescoes. The pottery and vases that were discovered in the ancient city were on exhibit in Santorini and Athens museums.

Our coaches departed Akrotiri, descending hairpin curves to Athinos Port. We boarded a large sailboat and sailed away on this sunny, beautiful day. The Santorini blue water was miles deep and my view of the island as we set sail was thrilling. A lovely family adopted me for the day, Joy and Phil (Joyful), grandparents who were spending a holiday with their granddaughter who had flown in from Brussels.

We sailed to Nea Kameni Volcano and climbed up 426 feet, past barren lava, to the summit. What a trek! I was almost at the top when the trail narrowed and I began to feel breathless and dizzy. I took my time descending, taking pictures and enjoying the view. Getting on and off the boat was tricky. We had to crawl over all the other boats anchored near the dock, and we had to repeat this process in order to reach our boat.

After we explored this natural phenomenon, we sailed toward Palia Kameni Island for a swim in the hot sulfur springs. I stripped to my suit and got in the coldest water that I had ever experienced. I had just sweated buckets at the volcano, so the water felt icy. I had to watch out for the huge rocks as I swam. Thanks to the help of a life preserver I made it to the springs. The exertion was exhilarating and worth the effort it took to return to the boat.

We sailed on to the slow-paced island Thirasia where we relaxed and enjoyed a delicious lunch. I ordered my favorite Greek dish, Mousaka (eggplant and potato).

Now it was time to visit Oia, a gorgeous gem with lovely vistas, picturesque streets, and beautiful sunsets. No one had warned me about the difficult climb up to the volcano or the long swim to the hot springs (optional), and now I had a much more difficult obstacle, getting up to the town of Oia. People either climbed the stairs or rode a donkey up the sheer cliff. I have NEVER seen anything (that I must ascend) that was so steep. I walked up several steep steps to the donkey and could hardly catch my breath. A young woman had refused to ride my donkey (notice that I am already identifying with this animal), feeling that he was too aggressive. He was the only donkey available at this point. So I tried to climb on. It became apparent, after two attempts, that I did not know what I was doing. The Greek guide knew no English and was determined that I should be properly seated before we began our long trek. He kept motioning with his hands while 19 properly-seated adults waited, staring at me, anxious for me to assume the proper posture so that we could be on our way. The guide became frustrated, raising his voice and increasing his motions. The angle and slope that we were on did not help. I leaned forward and he was happy.

We began to queue up, as the English would say, nose to tail, and our guide gave the command that everyone start. I had my heavy purse and a black bag with swim stuff and water bottle. One bag slung one way and one the other and I fought to grasp them while holding on to the reins of the donkey. All of my thoughts now centered on the poor animal (more identification). He had just been rejected as too unruly and now I was on his back. Having been a guidance counselor, I tried to make amends for my awkward attempts to right myself. I started to stroke his neck and spoke softly to him in my most gracious manner because he literally held my life in balance. It turned out that he did not like his position in the line-up. He wanted to be first or, at the very least, pass the donkey in front of him. So at every opportunity, he would try to close in. This caused extra shifting in a very precarious, close, high place. DO NOT ever call a donkey stupid, not when I am around. The guide knew exactly how to control them. The donkeys knew what every grunt, call, command and sound meant. They were wonderfully obedient.

Directly behind me was the young lady who had rejected my donkey. She sobbed uncontrollably all the way up, stopping only to apologize to her husband, crying, "I'm so sorry". He tried to soothe his wife saying that it was all right. She hysterically cried, "I am going to fall down this cliff". So much for a smooth beginning in their relationship. I felt very sorry for her and my composure began to waiver. I had never seen anyone so gripped and paralyzed with fear. I knew that I must pray and not look down. As we neared the top, the climb became too steep for the donkeys and the guide told us to get off. We walked (crawled) the rest of the way up. I was so grateful to see Oia, the village on the rim.

After I had explored this enchanting town and snapped many pictures, I stopped to rest. A tall young woman sat down beside me. We exchanged a few casual comments and she remarked that she was vacationing with friends. Her English was perfect, though she was from Germany. She seemed in no hurry, content to chat and enjoy the view with me. I occasionally broke the silence with a thought that I wanted to express. She looked at me with depth that I could not explain. We laughed and enjoyed the joy and serenity in our communion. I felt at peace. You may think, "Well, you've had a harrowing day and you were dreaming". I would agree EXCEPT that I had prayed that God would grant me safety and surround me with caring people on this trip. I think that she was an angel. What do you think?

It was so neat to walk out of my front door and see Fira, the island capital of Santorini. After a ten-minute brisk walk, I was downtown in the midst of a vacationer's delight. There were scores of shops hiding around every corner where I purchased hats, dresses, postcards, and jewelry. There were so many jewelry stores that it was difficult to make a choice. While exploring Fira, I was fascinated with the manner in which the free-form buildings were linked together. I visited the Museum of Prehistoric Thera that established Akrotiri as one of the most important Aegean centers during the 18th century. Their wall paintings, pottery and figurines were noteworthy.

Actually, the best feature of Fira was their bus station. After checking the posted schedule, I bought a ticket, and found the bus to Pyrgos, a must see for an artist. The bus ride was interesting, as everything was on this island. The driver was good looking with long, curly hair and the ticket collector was short-tempered and short on answers because of his limited English. I felt certain that I was the only American on the bus and I was happy that I had learned a few simple phrases. Their smiles and appreciation were a nice reward.

Pyrgos retained its medieval features, forming a white maze with splashes of blue and yellow. Each path held a secret. I explored for hours and saw only locals. I was prepared with sketching pencils, paper, kneaded erasure, cheese sandwich and water. I stopped to take a picture of a lovely entryway, with stairs leading up to a red door, flanked by flowers and a black cat. I snapped a picture, planning to use it as a reference to complete my painting when I returned home. Then I settled down to sketch the scene. After I finished, the front door of the house opened and an elderly Greek lady stepped out. She appeared to be very strong, probably due to climbing so many stairs in Pyrgos. I showed her the picture that I had just sketched of her home and asked if I could take her picture. She appeared to be flattered, nodded her head, and posed for me. Not only was I sketching her home, but I also wanted the owner's picture. Because tourists were rare and this situation had probably not occurred before, she seemed overwhelmed with happiness. She grabbed me, hugging and kissing me several times. She pointed toward her doorway smiling, nodding, and saying, "Tea, tea?" She was asking me into her home for tea.

Her home was so overwhelmingly different. As I sat waiting for her to prepare the tea, I could see into all of the rooms. Pictures were everywhere of the priest, her children, grandchildren, and Jesus. There were many crosses, especially in the bedroom. Suddenly she appeared with the tea (which was the strongest I have ever tasted) and sweets. She had proudly placed them on her finest serving tray along with water in her best glass. THEN a very strange thing happened. She grabbed a bag in the kitchen that appeared to contain vegetables and abruptly left without a good-bye!

I knew that her husband was eating in the kitchen because I had heard him and his wife exchange cross words. I think that he was scolding her for bringing a stranger into their home. Then a wave of panic swept over me as I remembered seeing a key on the outside of the front door. What if I were Gretchen, lured into this cottage for a "bad purpose"? I got up quickly, said "Efharesto" (thank-you) and bolted for the door. You cannot imagine my relief when I turned the knob and the front door opened. My finished watercolor painting is titled, "Tea in Santorini".

I continued sketching and exploring until the light began to fade, then made my way down through the maze to the town square bus stop. After I was seated on the bus, the ticket collector stuck his hand out for my ticket. I handed it to him and he angrily threw it over his shoulder onto the floor, shouting, "One way". I fumbled in my pocket for more Euro, suppressing a smile. What a funny attempt to tell me that my receipt from my previous trip was not a return ticket.

After requesting Angie and Mario to call the "Far & Wide" driver to pick me up, I thanked them for their help.

It was difficult to leave Santorini, but I was anxious to return home with my sketches and photos, so that I could attempt to recreate the magnificent beauty of Santorni in my watercolors. The flight to Athens was late, but I had reservations at the Airport Sofatel Hotel across the street, so I was not concerned. I had splurged on this five star hotel because of its convenience. The next morning I flew to Gatwick Airport in London, staying in an inexpensive, nearby guesthouse that offered free transportation and breakfast. The shuttle was outside the airport and I was fortunate to meet another passenger staying at the guesthouse who offered to help me with my luggage.

On my way home I thought about what I had learned and realized that it was to trust God. I remembered listening to the wind howl, banging the shutters on my apartment in Fira, yet peacefully drifting off to sleep. I thought about looking out of my airplane window at the old propeller on the Olympic plane taking me to Santorini, trusting it to deliver me to my destination safely. How much more, should I trust my Heavenly Father who created the heaven and the earth and all that is in it. Yes, I put my full trust in God, as I had not done before. I was never alone on this trip; I had a constant companion.

THE BEST IS YET TO COME…….

Trip 10
Sedona, Arizona

Hike to Sugarloaf Mountain

In my Exploritas program, I read about multi-activity involving yoga, tennis, and hiking. Northern Arizona University in Sedona was offering this opportunity. I presented the information to my tennis group and five of my friends agreed that it would be fun. Mary Bell took care of the organization and I shopped at a travel store for a hat that would provide protection from the sun and a trekking pole to assist in mountain climbing. We packed our sunscreen, hiking, and tennis gear with great expectations.

Sedona was a fabulous location for hiking. Our first meeting was held in the conference room at our motel. We met everyone in our group and were introduced to our leader. Dave, a professor at Northern Arizona University, was our hiking guide and supplied us with nutritional snacks for our hikes.

An early breakfast got us off to a good start. Our first hike was the Broken Arrow area. Dave was familiar with the vegetation and knew the names of each plant and flower. That afternoon we journeyed to the Sedona Racquet Club for orientation and an introduction to the master professional tennis coach. After some warm-up drills, we played several sets. It was difficult to concentrate on tennis while surrounded by the beauty of the mountains. In the evening those of us who could stay awake watched a "Sedona Film History".

Bright and early the next morning, we departed for

a beautiful chapel perched on top of a nearby mountain. In this inspirational setting, we practiced yoga stretching exercises. After one hour, we left promptly for Schuerman Mountain for our second hike. My friend Dede commented that she was enjoying the trip so much that she hoped I would discover another adventure for our group. The evening was free, so we found a marvelous restaurant with, you guessed it, a marvelous view. We were ready to kick back with a glass of our favorite wine.

The third day, our hike to the Soldier Heights area was longer, lasting three hours. In the afternoon we explored Sedona and enjoyed shopping for jewelry, among other treasures. We had fun after dinner listening to "Cowboy Songs & Ballads" by two of their local entertainers.

Yes, once again, the next day, we did the yoga stretching for athletes and, after that, hiked the Airport Vortex. In the afternoon we had competitive tennis matches with our twelve players. That evening, while watching the movie, "Broken Arrow", we began dropping like flies, unable to keep our eyes open.

Our final hike to Sugarloaf Mountain was exciting because of the challenge and difficulty. We literally had to give each other a hand as we climbed higher and higher. Dave had hinted that there would be a surprise at the final summit. Indeed there was! As we made our way through the thick underbrush, we were surprised to discover a ledge directly over our heads. We carefully climbed up to the ledge and were amazed to see a cave in front of us. We discovered markings on the walls of the cave, and Dave related the background history to us.

At this point, Dave directed us to a lovely clearing nearby. The view of God's magnificent nature surrounding us and the small village stretching out below us filled me with a quiet peace and a sense of accomplishment. There were flat rocks to sit on in the cleared area and Dave passed out paper and pencil, asking us to record our thoughts. This still time of contemplation was a welcomed opportunity. Afterward, we shared our discoveries about the past week. We had not expected a graduation ceremony, but Dave awarded us with diplomas accompanied by a hug. Our adventure had ended with a grand finale. We would never forget Sugarloaf Mountain and our awesome outdoor fun shared with special friends.

THE BEST IS YET TO COME…….

Trip 11
THE BEST OF FRANCE

Melissa Faye and Daphne Faye go to France

Many people said, “You’re going abroad with your granddaughter when America is at war?” Everyone said, “You’re going to France when Americans are renaming French fries?” Trafalgar said, “The trip may be cancelled.” Our daughter Cindy and her husband Dave (Melissa’s parents) said, “We will have to think about it.” Delta said, “We will charge you $200 for any change in flight plans.” I said, “Melissa’s high school graduation comes once in a lifetime.”

Suzy Grumelot, a friend of mine in charge of church planting in Paris, was helpful. She emailed information concerning the reticence factor for Americans in regard to traveling to France. She advised that common courtesies go a long way. She was right; the French people that we met were kind and helpful. She warned us of places to avoid and, best of all, places to shop. Galleries Lafayette and Le Printemps, near the Opera, were exciting, upscale, and stocked everything.

Melissa had a difficult transition because of jet lag, missing her family and friends, culture shock, and ageism. Worst of all, though we searched and searched, we could not find chips or pretzels. We did discover that Melissa and I were survivors and we began to value each other. God kept us safe and blessed us in many ways.

Our first day was a marathon, including the Louvre and Museum d'Orsay, prompted by free admission on Sunday. Our favorites were: *The Lacemaker* by Vermeer, *The Wedding Feast at Cana, The Winged Victory, The Dying Slave* by Michelangelo, *Venus de Milo, Adoration des Bergers, Saint Joseph Charpentier, Sacre de Napoleon,* and *Mona Lisa.*

ELIZABETH

I met Elizabeth on my first night in Paris. Our Trafalgar group was checking into our hotel when she approached me, saying that she thought that she was on the wrong tour. She appeared fearful and lost and asked me what city she was in. After many telephone calls, the clerk at the desk and I learned that Elizabeth was on the right tour. I assured her that Paris was correct and proceeded to write her room number and time of departure on an envelope for her. The next morning, I noticed her in the hotel restaurant and she appeared to be fine.

Well, she was not fine. When our tour group

was ready to depart the town that we had been visiting that day, Elizabeth was nowhere to be found. We fanned out and searched for her. Giles reported her missing to Trafalgar, the Visitor Center, and the police. Much later she was reported to be miles out of town visiting with a family. When our bus drove up to the house to pick her up, Elizabeth hugged each person and waved good-by to them. You would have thought that the strangers were Elizabeth's relatives.

When she rejoined our group I sat across the aisle from her and we had a lengthy conversation. Elizabeth showed me her passport and cash in paper bags in her purse. We discussed safety and the importance of holding on to your belongings. She confided that she was a widow with one son who did not speak to her because of a misunderstanding about some property. Elizabeth revealed that she had been traveling with Trafalgar for years, going from one tour to the next. Each time we stopped to see a sight, she would tell me, "I've been here; I've seen this before." When we returned to the hotel I passed this information on to Giles, remarking that I believed Elizabeth was in the first stages of Alzheimers.

Everything changed after this incident; we all took her under our wing and tried to protect her, especially Giles. A few days later she hurt her leg and Giles sent for a doctor, who dressed and bandaged her infection. Her leg was not healing properly so the doctor would not allow

> her to return to Scotland. Trafalgar paid a nurse to fly from Scotland to Paris. The nurse cared for her until her leg healed and she was ready to return home. Trafalgar refunded Elizabeth's money for her remaining tours.

The best thing about the entire trip was our tour director Giles from Bath, England. He was very young and Melissa immediately liked him. She would eagerly hop off the bus, hoping to stand next to Giles. Our trip began with a drive southwards into Burgundy wine country via its capital, Dijon, to the medieval town of Beaune. We sampled some regional wine and enjoyed a dinner of Lyonnaise specialties.

We boarded our local coach and drove to St Paul de Vence and Eze Village nestled in the hillside. We enjoyed stunning views of castles and countryside, with visits to Roque Gageac and Saint-emilion. We especially enjoyed St Paul de Vence, built high into the south-facing rock cliffs in a bend of the River Dordogne. While our group shopped in the little town, Melissa, Giles, and two other group members kayaked down the River Dordogne.

Our scenic drive through the Province of Van Gogh, decorated in lavender, brought us to the French Riviera and Nice. Melissa and I had great fun shopping in Nice and occasionally spotted a topless sunbather.

We enjoyed a taste of the high life on a visit to the Principality of Monaco to see the famous Monte Carlo casinos. The Casinos opened the door to magic and a unique atmosphere. Adding to the glamour, the city was preparing for the Grand Prix, one of the most prestigious motor races in the world. I felt like I was on a movie set, partially because of the life-like mannequins, seated on the benches or walking out of the restaurants. Bounded by the mountains and the sea, with its perfectly manicured lawns, the Principality of Monaco is well known the world over. Princess Grace of Monaco's portrait in the palace was stunning. The palace was complete with eighteen cannons and the changing of the guards.

We continued this fairy tale trip through Cannes where stars fulfilled their destiny on this fabled, fabulous, fairy-tale-like stretch of the Riviera. As we approached the walled city of Carcassonne, it began to rain in torrents. Of course, our raincoats and umbrellas were carefully packed in our suitcases in the storage area under the bus. We decided that this would be our only chance to see the ancient city, so we made the most of it. We trudged through the rain, scampering from overhang to overhang. When we reached our hotel, we were soaked. We had to depend on the hairdryer for our shoes as well as our hair.

Mont St. Michael, a town and an abbey first appeared as a distant, gray, rough-cut diamond set in the silver sea. They were improbably perched on a rock off the coast of Normandy. Many physical elements contributed to its remarkable effect, such as a 456-foot-high high spire topped by a gold-plated bronze statue of St. Michael that had been frequently struck by lightening. Ninth century chapels, the Gothic choir, and the cloister seemed suspended in midair, overlooking the surrounding tidal surges and quicksand far below. The experience was one of exhilaration as we beheld this evocative masterpiece. Melissa and I were breathless when we reached the top, both from exertion of climbing and exhilaration of this memorable experience.

Our next destination, the Basilica on top of St. Bernadette's Grotto, was more somber. Melissa filled a water bottle with the holy spring water to take back home for a family friend who had a cancerous tumor of the brain. That afternoon we boarded an antique train in Biarritz on the Spanish border that took us past wild sheep and ponies toward the Pyrenees to the summit of La Rhune Mountain. In a restaurant on the summit, we enjoyed the best hot chocolate in the world topped with Baileys. After a rest at our hotel we drove deep into the heart of the most famous wine region in the world, stopping at Margaux Lascombes to sample their wines.

We continued north to the Loire Valley where we visited the exciting Palace of Chenonceau, dating back to the period of Francois 1, King of France. We could still read inscriptions on the walls left by Queen Mary Stuart's Scottish guards. The 16th century Brussels tapestry was lovely with its original green color. During the First World War, a hospital occupied the Chateau's rooms. The garden was so large that 130,000 bedding plants were needed each spring.

The Normandy American Cemetery was laid out in the form of a Latin cross with 9,333 graves marked with identical white crosses conveying an unforgettable, tragic loss of life. The inscription on a marble table in the chapel inspired me: I GIVE UNTO THEM ETERNAL LIFE AND THEY SHALL NEVER PERISH.

We visited the Bayeux Tapestry Museum and enjoyed an elegant dinner at a lovely chateau that evening. Early the next morning, we stopped at Giverny to visit the house and gardens of Claude Monet's inspiration for his "water lily' paintings.

Melissa was so excited when we returned to Paris because I had promised her that we would shop until we dropped and that is exactly what we did. My map was not according to scale, so the policemen gathered around Melissa trying to point out the best way for us to locate her selected stores. The policemen were delighted to assist her and, when Melissa flashed her smile and nodded her blonde head, they beamed. After shopping, I decided that we would take a quick taxi ride (instead of the subway) back to the hotel in order to be ready for our four-course dinner that evening. Our last night in Paris proved to be a huge success. Some of us enjoyed the wine so much that we tangoed in a long line around the cabernet room. The show was lively with musicians singing Old French songs in a delightfully, bawdy manner. The costumes were ornate, in typical topless Parisian fashion. Our evening ended with an illuminated coach tour of Paris, driving down the Avenue des Champs Elysees and stopping in front of the l'Arc de Triomphe for pictures.

Au Revoir to Paris and France, our wonderful memories will live forever! If Melissa's memory fades, she can always look at her paintings (her portrait, Giverny Gardens, and Claude Monet's home) that her Nana painted for her.

Daphne Faye and Melissa Faye

THE BEST IS YET TO COME…….

Trip 12
Best of Britain

Shakespeare and Beatrix Potter

I could not believe that I was embarking on a 2,500 mile European trip that would take me from London all the way up to Isle of Skye in Scotland. I was a little disappointed that my roommate could not go at the last minute, but I had traveled alone on other trips so I anticipated a great adventure.

As we landed in London, I thought of Samuel Johnson's quote, "The man who tires of London, tires of life. For there is in London, all that life can afford." I had not gone to the luxury department store Harrods on my last two trips to England and was determined to make this my first stop. I was surprised to see the large variety of restaurants, 28 to be exact, serving everything from high tea to tapas to pub food.

The children's department was amazing. There was a Two Seater Mercedes SL for £9,995 and a Hummer for £21,995 for young children!

The next item that took my breath away was a shrine in the basement, directly in front of the descending escalator. Since the deaths of Diana, Princess of Wales, and Dodi

Fayed, Mohamed Al Fayed's son, Al Fayed had erected this memorial. It consisted of photographs of the two behind a pyramid-shaped display that held a wine glass smudged with lipstick from Diana's last dinner, as well as what was described as an engagement ring Dodi purchased the day

before they died. Al Fayed sold Harrods in 2010 to Qatar Holdings.

I could not resist this trivia. In 1898, Harrods debuted England's "first moving staircase". Nervous customers were offered brandy at the top to revive them after their ordeal. In 2007, Harrods hired a live Egyptian cobra to protect the shoe counter, guarding a £84,880 pair of haute couture ruby – sapphire and diamond – encrusted sandals launched by designer Rene Caovilla.

Our morning sightseeing tour included Westminster Abbey and St Paul's Cathedral. I disliked the new Gherkin's glass-domed building rising above the beautiful Cathedral. We took time out to watch the practice parade for Her Majesty the Queen's Birthday. The official birthday was marked each year by a colorful and historic military parade, known as Trooping the Color. The 1st Battalion Irish Guards, The Horse Guards, Massed Bands, Pipes and Corps of Drums, Kings Troop and Royal Horse Artillery arrived on parade. They marched to the traditional tune, "The British Grenadiers". I was informed that the empty carriage would carry Her Majesty the Queen, accompanied by His Royal Highness The Prince Philip, Duke of Edinburgh, to Buckingham Palace where there would be a Royal Salute and Royal Air Force aircraft flying past on her official birthday. It was awesome to observe a ceremony that had been in existence since 1748.

We visited the unmistakable 5,000-year-old monoliths of Stonehenge. They were the most important prehistoric sites in the British Isles, unique and like nothing else in the world. Our next town was lovely Cornwall, where spring flowers covered the cliffs and delighted the eye. We arrived in Plymouth on a beautiful sunny day and I took pictures of many "paintable" scenes. We could not miss the large stone beside the water that read, "Mayflower 1620".

Bath was famous for its Abbey that contained 56 scenes in the life of Jesus Christ. The Tintern Abbey in Wales, located on a riverbank in the wooded Wye Valley, was a fitting background for this medieval abbey. England's Lake District was immortalized by William Wordsworth when he described the lake water reflecting pastoral harmony, "The influences of light and shadow upon the sublime and the beautiful". Beatrix Potter's Hill Top Farmhouse, where she bred prize sheep, was now operated by her descendents. It has been established as a National Park to protect it for future generations. Top Farmhouse, where she bred prize sheep, was now operated by her descendents. The 10,000-year-old Lake District was a celebration of people and nature working together.

I am a huge fan of Beatrix Potter who, as a young person, spent her summers in the Lake District collecting plants and small animals and drawing them. It was so delightful to browse through the stores and discover her many *Peter Rabbit* books and animals. Potter used her royalties to buy property in the Lake District and worked to preserve the natural and historical sites.

The massive sandstone walls of Chester provided a pleasant two-mile walk. Chester has changed its image from a 2,000-year-old fortress to a present day thriving center of commerce. The 13th century medieval abbey church was magnificent and the stalls in the quire were masterpieces of 14th century woodcarvers' art. A well-known feature of Chester is the Eastgate clock tower.

On a rainy morning in Grasmere, we stood beside the Wordsworth graves that read: "The acclaimed poet William

Wordsworth described Grasmere as The fairest place on Earth". I was reminded of his famous poem:

DAFFODIL

I wandered lonely as a cloud
That floats on high o'er vales and hills,
When all at once I saw a crowd,
A host of golden daffodils;
Beside the lake, beneath the trees,
Fluttering and dancing in the breeze.

Continuous as the stars that shine
And twinkle on the Milky Way,
They stretched on never-ending line
Along the margin of a bay:
Ten thousand saw I at a glance,
Tossing their heads in sprightly dance.
William Wordsworth, 1770-1850

We continued exploring the Lake District with a cruise on Lake Windermere and an exciting train ride. Before boarding, we watched the crew shovel coal for our trip. We anxiously peered around the bend, trying to spot the train in the fog and grew silent listening for the train whistle. Shortly, we happily climbed on board for an enjoyable experience.

We were near Scotland and I began reviewing my notes and peering out of my window. The landscape became rugged as we traveled past the banks of Loch Lomond and into The Trossachs National Park. We continued deep into the Highlands to Glencoe, where we saw the site of the famous massacre. Our cruise of Loch Lomond introduced us to fog, new scenery, and a new dialect – the Scottish accent. The sign above the captain's door read, "Keep yer hein doon". We all knew that the Loch Ness monster "Nessie" did not exist, but continued to scan the horizon just in case.

A remarkable scenic day began with a stop at Culloden Moor to see the site of the battle, which defeated the hopes of a Stuart Monarchy. A large engraved stone told the story: "The Battle of Culloden was fought on this moor April 1746. The graves of the gallant highlanders who fought for Scotland and Prince Charlie are marked by the names of their clans." We drove along the shores of Loch Ness, then over the sea to Skye. The stark beauty of these isles attracted hermits, visionaries, and all those who craved peace and isolation. Dunvegan Castle was our next stop, the historic seat of the Clan MacLeod.

We traveled over a narrow, concrete bridge to Balmoral Castle, the Royal Family's Scottish retreat. The bridge was so small that everyone had to get off the bus and walk over the bridge. Then we were off to tiny Crathie Parish Church, where Queen Elizabeth attended and Princess Anne was married. A member of the parish conducting the tour pointed out where each person in the royal family sat and confided that, when Prince Charlie married Camille in this church, the congregation cheered and sang with gusto as the organ played, "Charlie is my Darlin".

Edinburgh was a fascinating city, but the Scottish Show and dinner was even more fascinating. A few couples in our group wore their clan's tartan; and there was bagpipe music, a highland dance, and Scotland's national dish – haggis. Prestonfield's famous Haggis was served with the traditional accompaniments of bashed 'neeps and tatties'. Each of the four courses was served with special music, lighting, and flare. This first class event was titled, "The World Famous Taste of Scotland Scottish Show & Dinner at Historic Prestonfield". The show was held in a lavish mansion built in 1687 noted for its reputable guest list, such as Winston Churchill, Margaret Thatcher, Grace Kelly, Sean Connery, and Elton John.

When we returned to England, we stopped at a huge, tall rock that displayed the name Scotland on one side and England on the other. We had a photo opportunity to take a picture of a Scottish gentleman playing the bagpipe. As we continued our trip, I was surprised to see Hadrian's Wall built in 122 AD. We toured Lendal Tower in York and visited the shortest street, known in 1505 as "Whip – Ma – Whop – Ma – Gate".

The following day began with a scenic drive through the Midlands to Coventry, home of Lady Godiva, to see its old and new cathedrals. Our journey continued to Anne Hathaway's cottage at Stratford-upon-Avon with its old-fashioned gardens and orchard. The cottage walls were made of puddled mud and wattles finished with horsehair plaster. The cottage had the added attraction of being where Shakespeare came to woo his bride-to-be. Set on a beautiful river at the very heart of England, Stratford had the good fortune of having the birthplace and other properties as shrines for those who love and revere Shakespeare. All of the cottages and furnishings were in remarkably good condition and portrayed life as it was in 1564. Shakespeare was born and died in Stratford but spent most of his life in London, building a reputation as playwright and poet.

Our next excursion allowed us to explore Warwick, one of England's great medieval castles. The 1898 Royal Weekend Party was remarkably life-like. The wax figures gave the impression that you were looking in on the actual Royal Party. There was the nana with her white hat and apron holding a baby in a christening gown. There was a seated gentleman lighting his cigarette. Even more impressive, a lady was gazing into her full-length mirror at her new gown while a maid was kneeling on the floor pinning up her hem. Another maid was drawing a bath, bending over to feel the temperature of the water. In another room, a servant had just delivered a letter on a silver tray to the madam. I could continue, but I'm sure that you have the idea. We also visited the Armory and grim Dungeon.

After breakfast, we drove through the Cotswold Hills to Blenheim Palace, the birthplace of Sir Winston Churchill. Churchill's and his wife's gravesites were in a quiet neighborhood surrounded by lovely flowers. Our last stop, Oxford, was short, but interesting because of their university. The library and the round hall where the students received their diplomas were unique.

Yes, we had traveled 2,500 miles and seen much of Britain, beginning and ending in London. England had seemed very proper with its formal titles and protocol. Wales and Scotland were rugged and foggy with their cliffs and moors. The Scottish people appeared to have strong ties with their clan, tartans, colors, names, etc. Gallant highlanders were remembered and celebrated as if their battles were yesterday. The small Crathie Church was sweeter than the magnificent Westminister Abbey. While in Scotland, I felt that families were close and the quality of family life was valued. These were my fleeting impressions of my short trip and now it was time to bid farewell to Britain.

QUEEN'S BIRTHDAY PARADE

THE BEST IS YET TO COME…….

Trip 13
Florence, Italy

Montecatini Terme

We idealize Tuscany with good reason. When we travel there we do not take a short journey, but an endless one. Amid all the beauty, museums, history, and good food, we don't feel like a tourist; we feel like a part of the moment. The beauty is intoxicating and we wanted that feeling to last. The Tuscan wines and cuisine reflected a culture that made Tuscany unforgettable. Elizabeth Barrett Browning said it so well, "The air of this place seems to penetrate the heart...it draws you, raises you, excites you."

It was touch and go as to whether my good friend and neighbor, Dot, would be able to join me on this trip. She had been undergoing cancer treatments and needed her doctor's approval for this venture. She made her down payment and Delta promised full repayment if that became necessary. Fortunately, she got a good report from her doctor and we were elated.

Trinity College staffed our tour, "Classic Tuscany and the Treasures of Florence". Dot and I loved the idea of staying in a little town outside of Florence for two weeks. Montecatini Terme was known for its Terme water and mud baths. Their spa was luxurious, with a lovely open bar, restaurant, fountain, frescos and fine art. In the afternoon guests could relax in the soothing surroundings and enjoy piano concerts.

Dot and I arrived at Hotel Reale in the afternoon. When we opened the gate to the courtyard, Laura and Paula, our tour directors warmly welcomed us. We were just in time for the reception that included drinks and hors d'oeuvres. After our long journey, botched plane connections, and taxi ride, we gave a huge sigh of relief and heartily greeted everyone. We felt right at home and especially liked the location of our room one flight above the lobby. Posh shops and cafes, a marvelous bakery with every imaginable pastry, and a drugstore were within walking distance. We also discovered that Giuseppe Verdi was born in Montecatini Terme.

That evening, Paula presented a crash course titled, "Survival *Italiana*". The points that she stressed were that we must have *(pazienza)* patience and that Italians would not answer *si* or *no*, but that (*dipende*) depends. She said that Italians always put their best foot forward – *bella figura*, an Italian expression that summed it up quite nicely. It's an unspoken dress code ingrained in a culture where everybody makes a concerted effort to make a good impression.

DOT AND DAPHNE

Our hotel was family owned and the owner's family dined in the restaurant in the evening. I noticed that even the family's dog felt at home, sleeping under the hotel manager's desk. I liked the table set up for our bottles of wine and the salad bar that we could circle around and help ourselves before the main entrée. Dot, a retired librarian, was speechless when she came upon the hotel's great selection of books that afforded her the opportunity of continuing her routine of reading several books a week.

MONTECATINI TERME

Trinity College selected expert professors to inform us about the life and works of Florence's great artists. They guided our path shedding both light and lessons on the jumbled beauty of this great city. Our first lecture, by a professor at the British Institute, was on Italian Renaissance Sculpture. Of particular interest were Ghiberti's *Sacrifice of Isaac* and Donatello's *David.* The afternoon lecture on Early Renaissance was designed to prepare us for our trip to the Uffizi Museum, one of the most important museums in the world. Machiavelli, when describing this unique period in Western culture, said: "This province seems to have been born to give new life to dead things, as can be seen from its poetry, painting and sculpture." Botticelli who best captured the cultural climate, created *Birth of Venus, Primavera and Adoration of the Magi.* Leonardo Da Vince painted his magnificent *Annunciation* when he was just twenty-years-old, about the time that Michelangelo painted his first masterpiece, *Tondo Doni.*

On our field trip to Pisa's famous leaning tower, I learned that there was a double miracle: its static, impossible balancing, and its airy elegance. Slanting improbably into the heavens like a Tower of Babel, ringed by delicate rows of white arches, it was truly an architectural delight. The leaning beauty started to list as it was being built in the early twelfth century. Over the years there have been efforts to correct this leaning; the most recent has stabilized the structure – for the time being, at least.

The pulpit in Pisa's 13th century Baptistry was one of the best examples of the transition from Romanesque style to Gothic by Nicola Pisano. A large fresco that told the story of those who survived the bombs of World War II caught my eye. Its scene of Death riding across an apocalyptic landscape inspired Listz to compose his *Tortentanz* concerto.

DAVID

That afternoon we received instruction to prepare for a train ride into Florence the next day. The professors lectured on Florence and the Medici before The Golden Age and after. Key events included the Black Death and the death of Lorenzo. The evening lecture was about Florence and the Medici and The Granducal Period. Key events discussed were

The Prince by Machiavelli, Galileo appearing before the Inquisition, and the Dukes and Grandukes of Tuscany.

After our short train ride to Florence, we went to see Michelangelo's *David* at the Accademia. Words are not adequate to describe the magnificent elevated statue, so well placed in his own huge space. We observed him from a distance, an intense young man contemplating his task. Without doubt this figure has surpassed every other statue…such are the satisfying proportions and beauty of the finished work.

Our next stop was San Lorenzo and the Medici Chapels that contained the family tombs (decorated by Donatello and Lippi).

So much to see and so little time. I had read about Florence's pride, the Duomo, our last stop. The gorgeous cathedral housed two panoramic perches, one atop Giotto's belltower, the other at the summit of Brunelleschi's Dome. Brunelleschi came up with the ingenious double shell construction in 1420. The Baptistry: The *Gates of Paradise* depicted great depth in shallow relief. Michelangelo was reportedly so moved when he saw the magnificent *Gates* that he proclaimed they would grace the very gates of Paradise in Heaven.

We were up early to journey to Sienna, known for its Duomo, a hulking Gothic Cathedral. Sienna prides itself on 14th-century Sienese Masters who were able to help consolidate the supremacy of Tuscan art and boost its reputation. The floors and columns are magnificently designed. The Pisano pulpit is a masterpiece of Gothic carving.

The best thing about our day in Sienna was relaxing in the Piazza delCampo, one of Europe's loveliest squares. We were free to sample different foods, chat, and people watch.

It was nice to know that we were not expected to follow a planned agenda and that we could simply enjoy the moment. After chatting with a local we learned that Tuscany's most important festival, the "Palio", is held in Sienna each year. It would be great fun to watch the bareback horse races involving competitors from the neighborhoods. I could visualize the locals frenzied yelling and cheering for their favorite.

We enjoyed our second trip to Florence the next day to see Santa Croce, Florence's Westminster Abbey. The Gothic pantheon contains the tombs of Michelangelo, Machieavelli, Rossini, and Galileo (reburied in 1737). The renowned leather shop is located behind the Sacristy.

UFFIZI MUSEUM IN FLORENCE

Because crowds would be tight and tourists were expected to observe the art on their own, we received a final preparation for the Uffizi Museum. The professor gave us a map that detailed exact locations of each artist's works and tips on how we should proceed to locate them.

Our afternoon was free so Dot and I rode the funicular up to Montecatini Alto, set in a pretty medieval town. I took dozens of pictures of the picturesque flowers, doorways and houses. As we walked through the neighborhood, it was apparent that the residents took pride in their homes and landscaping. After we finished shopping, we found a delightful sidewalk café and enjoyed a Tuscan lunch.

MONTECATINI ALTO

Finally the day for our trip to the Uffizi Museum arrived. It was raining and as we approached Florence, I noticed a long line in front of the Museum. Our group was delighted to be ushered in through a side door, avoiding a lengthy wait. It was a thrilling, delicious moment, stepping into the Uffizi. I clutched my map that I had memorized, and floated in. We were about to see master-pieces that had endured for centuries and would remain forever. These were the moments that I could not put a price tag on or recreate. I just had to "seize the day" and bask in this golden opportunity.

In the afternoon Dot and I decided to go to the Pitti Palace, a one-time residence of the Medici family, containing royal apartments, Boboli Gardens, costumes, silverware, and porcelain. It housed Raphael's *La Velata* and Titian's *Mary Magdalene.* What a delicious assortment.

The next morning, we were off to the little town of Vinci where a bastard child named Leonardo was born, who grew up to become one of the greatest scientific minds and artistic talents in history. We viewed an exhibit in his museum that contained over forty models of mechanical building, flying and war machines that he had designed. Up the road, set in an olive-clad landscape, was his simple birthplace. Nearby was a plain small church with a baptistry built in the seventh century. The ancient font, mentioning his grandfather's name, in which Leonardo was baptized, had been preserved in the middle of an octagonal room.

We drove through beautiful Tuscan countryside to the Villa Rospigliosi for lunch. We drove up a very long hill until the road turned into dirt with tall bushes on either side hiding the view. At last we came upon a large driveway that approached a four-story Villa. When we caught our breath, we ascended the stairs up to a tall open doorway. Laura and Paula (elegantly dressed) greeted us and announced that we were in for some surprises. Inside was a table, laden with a delicious assortment of hors d'oeuvres. After enjoying our happy hour, they ushered us into the banquet room and when everyone was seated the room became dark and quiet. Four waiters brought in our flaming main course – pig on the spit. We were totally elated and applauded their efforts. After dinner, we walked around the grounds, enjoying the fountain and gazebo.

Returning to the villa, we were led into the conservatory (that resembled the Pitti Palace) for our second surprise. Clive Britton, renowned pianist, had flown to Florence to present us with a piano concert & lecture titled "Franz Liszt: The Italian Years". Britton presented selections from three volumes of music representing pilgrimages. He stated, "With the liberalization of the artistic atmosphere in Paris, it became the melting pot of romanticism. George Sand, Balzac, Delacroix, Victor Hugo, Dumas, Paganni, Rossini, Berlioz, Chopin were all among Liszt's close friends. Musicians and music began to be affected by other art forms and influences of the surrounding world." His final volumes represented aspects of Italian painting, sculpture, and literature and documented the birth of romanticism in music. We were transported beyond our surroundings to Villa d'Este and finally to *Lift Up Your Hearts*. Our travel guide, Laura, an opera buff, had invited Britton and we were eternally indebted to her for our memorable afternoon.

Lucca, a genteel city of opera, olive oil, and palace gardens, was our last city to visit. Puccini was born in Lucca and was celebrated in concerts in the sumptuous villas north of town. Magnificent walls surrounded their Duomo and San Michele in Forno. Chestnuts and umbrella pines shaded the gravely path on top of Lucca and provided a great view of palazzo gardens and the Apuan Alp.

Our farewell dinner was a mixture of joy and sadness. Yes, we had idealized Tuscany because the wonderful cypress trees and landscapes are unlike any other we had ever seen. We had been put under a spell of beauty. However, all things must come to an end. *Arrivederci* to Laura and Paula, Hotel Reale, Montecatini Terme, Florence, and Tuscany.

THE BEST IS YET TO COME…….

Recent Trips

California

My husband and I have friends who reside in Scottsdale, Arizona, and maintain a boat in Sausalita Marina in California. Bruce and I received an invitation to visit Susan and David and stay on their boat. We immediately replied yes, pleased at the thought of a new experience. When we arrived, pulled our suitcases down the boardwalk and stepped onto their boat, “Job Site”, we knew that we had made the right decision. The first thing that they wanted to show us was their neighbor’s revived waterfront folly of arabesque cupolas and colonnades recently featured in the *Architectural Digest*. The owner had constructed an overscale barge and christened it the “Taj”. William Harlan, a San Francisco Bay Area real estate developer, replicated the Taj Mahal with three levels comprising twelve rooms and 4,500 square feet flanked by a pair of screens at the entry. The opulent, beautifully decorated creation was remarkable. After seeing the sights with our good friends and celebrating Bruce’s birthday at The Palace Hotel, we said our goodbyes and continued our trip.

Our first stop was Yosemite Lodge where we stayed several days so that we could enjoy the park. From there we continued on to Monterey Bay and a visit to the Monterey Aquarium. We visited the Basilica at Caramel-By-the-Sea and enjoyed the 17-mile drive through one of the most beautiful residential enclaves in the world.

Our views and landscape changed when we turned onto Coastal Highway One (the Cabrillo Highway). It was a truly amazing and most spectacular road. Up to Big Sur the road meandered like some fantastic carnival ride. The Bixby Bridge, notable because of the 320-foot length of central span and the height of 260 feet above the creek, was remarkable. Big Sur is the centerpiece of Scenic Highway One with its endless view of the Pacific.

Our destination for the evening was San Simeon because it is located near Hearst Castle. In San Simeon we were amazed to see colonies of elephant seals sleeping on the shore. They looked ghastly because they were in the process of molting. Early the next morning, we drove to the Hearst Castle. I thought about how exciting it must have been in the early twentieth century to have a castle between Big Sur and Hollywood. I could imagine Marion Davies, Greta Garbo, Clark Gable, and Cary Grant driving to the castle for dining in the Refectory, swimming in the pool, chatting with Hollywood's famous directors and writers, watching their movies in the theatre, playing pool in the billiard room, and reading in the library. Well, I am getting too carried away, however; the Hearst Empire included newspapers, magazines, real estate, ranches, mines, radio stations, warehouses and castles. Everyone knew that the hilltop castle was a veritable warehouse of rare antiquities and architectural styles. It was appropriately named – Building On "The Enchanted Hill"

Alaska

Our Holland America Tour began in Fairbanks where we boarded the McKinley Explorer to Denali. On our first day we spotted a moose and a grizzly bear with her cubs. I thought, "What a strange place. Where else would we see a wolf walk down the road behind our bus and watch snowshoe hares in the grass?" Our next stop was Anchorage where Bruce enjoyed a glacier landing on Mt. McKinley.

Alyeska Resort was fabulous because of the tramway up to the Seven Glaciers Restaurant on top of Mt. Alyeska. I loved swimming in their Olympic pool and hiking on their great trails.

At last, we set sail on the Veendam from Seward. We were pleased with our cabin and balcony because of our close views of the glaciers and small towns. Bruce could set up his tripod and zoom in on his subjects without interference. This was our first cruise and we were delighted with the buffets, lectures, and entertaining musicals.

Bruce joined a Guides Choice Photo Discovery group in Haines and took a Photo Safari by Land and Sea in Juneau. A remarkable sight was the field of firewood blooms surrounded by the Mendenhall Glacier that originated in the Juneau Icefield.

Ketchikan, the Salmon Capital of the World, has great totems and jewelry bargains. We felt so rested after our cruise. It was especially nice to enjoy the perfected itinerary. I loved eating different, delectable food in any amount, at any time.

Alaska was so different. At 10 pm the sun was still shining on the snow-covered peaks. As we turned to the east we could still see the glacier spill from the mountains to the valley floor, its white surface crisscrossed with deep blue crevasses that seemed to swallow the light. As we watched, a piece of ice broke off a large glacier (called calving) and tumbled to the rocks below. A few moments later, we heard the crash, and its echo.

Alaska is famous for its spectacular scenery. There are mirrored lakes, tall waterfalls, rugged peaks, and soaring cliffs. Most of this beautiful landscape was created by thousands of glaciers, over thousands of years.

As we approached Vancouver, we stood on our balcony watching the large city come closer and closer, and suddenly we were on top of it; an abrupt end to a delightful journey.

Yellowstone National Park

Old Faithful & Yellow Bus/Moran

Our airplane landed in Jackson Hole in the evening and we had an opportunity to explore the art galleries. The studios provided an elegant venue for shoppers and collectors to view various crafts. The exclusive retailers have selected truly unique sculpture, paintings, and photography worth more than a second look. We stayed in Teton Village two nights, then we departed for Grant Village in Yellowstone.

As we drove into the Tetons we saw exquisitely beautiful peaks and landscape. Jeremy Schmidt said, "These are impossible mountains. Rock doesn't soar upward with such singular dominance, such gravity defying grace. The Tetons don't merely scrape the sky, they occupy it." Our elevation reached 7,733 as we approached Grant Village.

YELLOWSTONE PAINTING

Yellowstone National Park inspires awe in travelers from around the world. Yellowstone gives a glimpse of earth's interior with its waterfalls, lava flows, and thermal areas. Fire and ice forged Yellowstone. There are stark extremes of geysers and molten lava and the beauty of Yellowstone Lake and its lovely Victorian Hotel.

There is the fear of getting too close to a grizzly bear and the tenderness that you observe through your binoculars as you watch the mother bear frolic with her cubs.

In Hayden and Lamar Valley along a tranquil stretch of the Yellowstone River, the fields with the mountains in the background are pleasing and quiet. However, you can gaze through a telescope into that same valley and observe a wolf devouring an animal. The viewer is aware of the ravens circling above, looking for prey for the wolves, diving down, so the wolf will know the location of his next meal. Yellowstone is a harsh paradise. Another contrast is that of Old Faithful's predictability. However, the future is anything but predictable because of possible fires, earthquakes, and volcanic eruptions.

YELLOWSTONE PAINTING

The most amazing fact I learned about the park was that the fires of 1988 burned the light canopy of lodgepole pines letting in water and sunlight and allowing pine seedlings, grasses and wildflowers to flourish. I had previously thought that a fire was devastating. It took years of study for the geologists to agree with the positive outcome of the 1988 fire. As we drove through the mountains, we noticed a huge contrast of the dead, burned lodgepoles on the ground and the growth of new, green pine seedlings.

The Grand Canyon of Yellowstone is more than 20 miles long and over 1,000 feet deep. In the same area, we observed the contrasts of the turquoise beauty of "Morning Glory Pool" and the gray ugliness of "Artist Point Mudpots". It is weird to see the hot spots of steam in the Firehole River. One would think that the lovely river would be cool because it is icy blue. Yellowstone's grounds are so volatile that warning signs are everywhere. The ranger told us that it was not unusual for animals to be burned and die in their environment.

I liked the park rangers' presentations because they gave their audience an awareness about the park, wildlife, geology, and a distinct code of protection and preservation to pass down to future generations. There is pride in each of their presentations. Yellowstone is the world's first national park and largest, containing more than 2 million acres of geysers, lakes and waterfalls. All of the villages have Education Centers and offer a variety of engaging exhibits and films. Young college students from all over the world work in Yellowstone during the summer months. Conversely, retired couples park their mobile homes and serve in many different capacities. We encountered exuberant employees during our visit.

It was a thrill to stay in Old Faithful Inn with its warm glow and rich gnarled timbers. One of the most treasured features of the hotel is the 80-foot chimney, which hosts eight fireplaces. The four-story lodge bustled with guests, energy, and activity. The piano and violin music in the evening was soothing after a busy day. Sitting on the second story porch gave us an opportunity to watch the geyser and the tourists.

OLD FAITHFUL INN PAINTING

We departed Old Faithful early because our next destination was Mammoth at the North Entrance to Yellowstone. The imposing Roosevelt Arch, so named after its dedication by President Roosevelt in 1903, serves as the formal gateway to the park. The monument has been designated a World Heritage Site. The inscription on the Roosevelt Arch proclaims that these public lands have been set aside - FOR THE BENEFIT AND ENJOYMENT OF THE PEOPLE.

As we drove south through Lamar Valley I could see why Frommer dubbed it "The Serengeti of North America" for its wildlife. We had difficulty driving because of the bison crossing the roads. They came so close to our car that I could have touched one.

Canyon Village, our last stop in Yellowstone, was where Bruce and I experienced a "Wake Up to Wild Life Tour". The Yellow Bus that we toured in had quite a history. 2007 marked the long-awaited "homecoming" of eight vintage buses. The buses included 1930 vehicles that were originally part of the fleet. They still possessed the original canvas rollback tops for enhanced sightseeing opportunities. At 5:45 am we scraped the ice off our windshield so that we could drive to the pick-up destination. We enjoyed a boxed breakfast and coffee before climbing onto our Yellow Bus and covering up with a wool blanket that awaited us. Our driver enthusiastically informed us about the wild animals that we would see. After all, we were in prime "critter country". After telling us the story about the Yellow Bus, he asked us not to shut the doors and added that he would shut them. He appeared anxious to maintain Yellowstone's treasure and enhance our nostalgic ride.

Our guide was knowledgeable about roads and turnoffs to observe wildlife. He set up his powerful telescope at each stop and zoomed in on the animals. We would not have seen these invisible creatures without this tour. When it warmed up, he folded back the canvas top and we experienced an unforgettable panoramic view of Yellowstone. It amazed me to see the people flock to the animals clutching their cameras. Tourists would park in the middle of the road, jump out of their car, and yell, "What do you see?" If there were several cars parked in an area, oncoming traffic would stop and there would be a traffic jam. Rangers would appear out of nowhere and direct the traffic.

An outstanding artist of the Western scene is Thomas Moran. Moran's sketches influenced Congress to establish Yellowstone as the world's first national park in 1872. His pictorial analysis captured the area's unique imagery. I was anxious to see "Artist Point" that had inspired Moran to create his famous painting of the falls. We set our alarms to arrive early because of Frommer's statement that "Artist Point" was the most photogenic and photographed spot in the country. This statement proved to be true. Buses with tourists from all over the world filled the parking spots. Every couple wanted their picture taken in front of the falls. They would patiently line up and wait for their turn. I was filled with awe to think of Moran's discovery and beautiful painting.

Peter Hassrick wrote, "Moran knew immediately, as he stepped into the Yellowstone wilderness, that its sublime forms and chromatic splendor represented more than mere subject for the painter's brush. Here was material so resplendent with natural spectacle and singular beauty that it became at once a regional and a national symbol. So epic were the perceived dimensions of grand scenes like the Lower Falls, Yellowstone Lake, and the various geyser basins that they were readily transformed into symbols of an expansive national dream. Expressly, they met the aspirations of many Americans to possess and boast of something indigenously and inherently superior to Europe . . . something for which Americans could stay home."

Our last night was spent in Jackson Hole at an Alpine Inn Bed and Breakfast. When we wearily drove up to the Inn, I spotted a lovely garden filled with flowers. After checking in, Bruce and I helped ourselves to tea and freshly baked chocolate-chip cookies. We "de-stressed" in their rocking chairs overlooking the garden. Finally, hunger overcame us and we enjoyed a pasta dinner at an Italian restaurant across the street. We were not anxious to return to our busy lifestyle of television, computer, and hectic schedules. We would miss the cool weather, nature, and beauty of the West.

REMEMBER, THE BEST IS YET TO COME!

The author can be reached via email:

daphnef@cfl.rr.com

9 780692 011690

LaVergne, TN USA
26 November 2010
206193LV00002B/2/P

9 780692 011690